PUBLIC POLICY AND MENTAL HEALTH

Other Books in the Prevention Practice Kit

For Peter and Ellen Pirog, the best parents and grandparents ever.

PUBLIC POLICY AND MENTAL HEALTH

Avenues for Prevention

MAUREEN A. PIROG
Indiana University, University of Washington

EMILY M. GOOD
Indiana University - Bloomington

Los Angeles | London | New Delhi
Singapore | Washington DC

Los Angeles | London | New Delhi
Singapore | Washington DC

FOR INFORMATION:

SAGE Publications, Inc.
2455 Teller Road
Thousand Oaks, California 91320
E-mail: order@sagepub.com

SAGE Publications Ltd.
1 Oliver's Yard
55 City Road
London EC1Y 1SP
United Kingdom

SAGE Publications India Pvt. Ltd.
B 1/I 1 Mohan Cooperative Industrial Area
Mathura Road, New Delhi 110 044
India

SAGE Publications Asia-Pacific Pte. Ltd.
3 Church Street
#10-04 Samsung Hub
Singapore 049483

Acquisitions Editor: Kassie Graves
Editorial Assistant: Elizabeth Luizzi
Production Editor: Brittany Bauhaus
Copy Editor: QuADS Prepress (P) Ltd.
Typesetter: C&M Digitals (P) Ltd.
Proofreader: Jeff Bryant
Indexer: Diggs Publication Services, Inc.
Cover Designer: Glenn Vogel
Marketing Manager: Lisa Sheldon Brown
Permissions Editor: Adele Hutchinson

Copyright © 2013 by SAGE Publications, Inc.

Printed in the United States of America

Library of Congress Cataloging-in-Publication Data

Public policy and mental health : avenues for prevention / editors, Maureen A.

Pirog, Emily M. Good.

p. cm. — (Prevention practice kit)
Includes bibliographical references and index.

ISBN 978-1-4522-5802-7 (pbk.)

1. Mental illness—Prevention—Government policy.
2. Preventive mental health services. I. Pirog, Maureen A. II. Good, Emily M.

RA790.5.P83 2013
362.19689—dc23   2012040376

This book is printed on acid-free paper.

SUSTAINABLE FORESTRY INITIATIVE
Certified Chain of Custody
Promoting Sustainable Forestry
www.sfiprogram.org
SFI-01268
SFI label applies to text stock

12 13 14 15 16 10 9 8 7 6 5 4 3 2 1

Brief Contents _____

Detailed Contents _____

1   Introduction to Public Policy and Prevention

When we think of public policies, our minds turn to constitutions, laws, regulations, treaties, judicial interpretations, funding priorities, and the public authority to implement these various policies. More broadly, public policy really deals with all aspects of the publics' authority to make decisions across a wide spectrum of topics, including, among others, equity and fairness, economic, criminal, and psychosocial issues. Policies can be far-reaching, including international treaties, trade agreements and embargos, international aid, emergency management, or national defense. Within our borders, they can focus on taxation, medical care, education, occupational licensure, and the focus of this book, the prevention of mental illness and the promotion of health.

But public policies do not fall like manna from the heavens. They are developed through processes that are political, legal, and administrative. While the initial expectation may be that a program or policy or law may be beneficial, the reality can fall short of expectations. The *Journal of Policy Analysis and Management*, which publishes high quality evaluations of public programs, amply demonstrates that many public programs have failed due to poor design, environmental conditions, or implementation deficiencies.

Assessing the likely or realized impacts of public laws, programs, policies, or administrative procedures is the domain of public policy analysis. Specifically, policy analysis is the systematic assessment of policy alternatives to a particular public problem or issue. The policy analysis tool kit is extensive and includes, among others, evaluability assessment, process or implementation studies, social experimentation and program evaluation, cost–benefit analysis, forecasting, risk assessment, efficiency modeling, and constrained optimization methods such as linear or multiobjective goal programming. The Association for Public Policy Analysis and Management is the professional organization for public policy researchers and over 100 schools of public affairs produce policy analysts.

The extent to which public policies influence practice, attitudes, and behaviors is at the heart of policy analysis. However, rather than emphasizing the mechanics of the tools of policy analysis, this volume provides an overview of how public policies are developed and how these policies can and have influenced practice, attitudes, and behaviors in the mental health arena. For example, in 1975, the U.S. Congress passed the Education for All Handicapped Children Act (Public Law 94-142). This act required all public schools accepting federal funds to provide equal access to education for children with physical and mental disabilities. The origins of this act are found in the Civil Rights Movement and the *Brown v. Board of Education* (1954) decision. While this decision extended equal protection under the law to minorities, it also paved the way for similar gains for those with disabilities including mental health problems. Grassroots advocacy efforts and legal actions by parents on behalf of their children can be traced back to 1933. Parents were the primary impetus in the struggle to improve educational opportunities for developmentally challenged children (U.S. Department of Education, 2011).

While the nuts and bolts of policy analytical methods are not the focus of this book, the process of policy analysis bears some discussion because it relates not only to policy analysis but also to policy development and advocacy, which can be of great interest to mental health counselors. The basic steps of policy analysis are depicted in Figure 1.1.

Some of these steps can be broken into subparts. For example, Bardach (2005) includes assembling evidence or data as a separate step in policy analysis, although it is discussed here as part of the problem definition

Figure 1.1   Steps of Policy Analysis

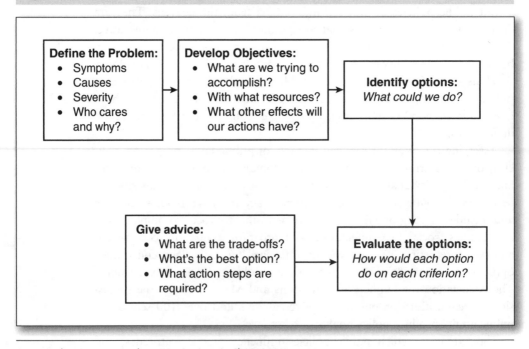

Source: Klatwitter (personal communication, April 15, 2011).

(*Editors' note:* For more on problem definition and related steps in a general approach to program development and evaluation in prevention, refer to Book 7 in this *Kit*). More general descriptions and perspectives on the policy analysis process can be found in Stokey and Zeckhauser (1975), Bardach (2005), Lejano (2006), and Weimer and Vining (2011).

Step 1: Define the Problem

Problem definition sounds deceptively easy. Now suppose you are a counselor worried about drug addiction. Is the problem the easy availability of prescription or illegal drugs, a drug culture, poor enforcement of drug laws, or something else? Because this counselor started with a huge issue, let's narrow the scope a bit and assume she believes that marijuana is too easily accessible and the rates of use of this drug by middle school children are too high. She considers marijuana a gateway drug that leads to the eventual use of more pernicious drugs as children become older. Figure 1.1 depicts the steps involved in policy analysis.

One might legitimately ask *why* we should view marijuana use by middle school children as a *public* problem meriting remedies using public dollars when the maladaptive behavior of children is usually viewed as a private, parental responsibility. This is always a critical question to pose. In this case, one could argue that marijuana distribution and use is illegal and the fact that this happens at all is a failure of our legal system. Additionally, public schools should not only educate children but also safeguard their safety. Widespread use of illegal drugs by children while under the supervision of public school employees suggests another failure of a public organization. Another possibility is that drug use is creating distractions in classrooms, limiting the ability of teachers to conduct their primary mission of education. One more possibility is that drug use may be more heavily concentrated in schools with low-income or minority children. If this can be demonstrated, then one could additionally argue that public schools are not providing equal protection for poor or minority children. Any and all of these are legitimate reasons to move this issue into the public domain.

If marijuana use by middle school children is the problem under consideration, then a policy analyst would want to document the severity of the problem. How widespread is this problem? When do children start smoking marijuana? How many are using this drug by age 10, 12, or 13? Are these children experimenting with this drug once, or are they frequent users? It is important to use the best available data and then calibrate your answers. Let's say hypothetically that based on random drug tests, survey responses, or administrative counseling records, we believe that one third of eighth graders have smoked marijuana, although the truth could lie between 25% and 40%. Based on the same sources of data, we believe that 10% to 15% of eighth graders are regular users of this drug.

Most parents, school administrators, and public officials would be alarmed if drug use figures among middle school children were this high. But in terms of stressing why this public problem should take precedence over the myriad other public problems like hunger, homelessness, and domestic violence, the analyst would have to make a case that the consequences of illegal drug use among middle school children has important and negative societal ramifications. Drug use might lead to disruptions in classrooms, resulting in lower quality education for all students. Children who smoke marijuana may not exercise good judgment and may harm themselves as well as others. If it can be demonstrated that marijuana is a gateway drug leading to other drugs with even more harmful health outcomes, then the public health costs of medical treatment and drug rehabilitation for this group could become a factor. A cost–benefit analysis would point to the negative consequences of drug use, including increased costs of law enforcement and incarceration, increased public health care and drug rehabilitation costs, time lost at work by parents, and so on. It is up to the policy analyst to make the case that the problem is sufficiently serious that it warrants public attention.

It should be noted that many public agencies collect and maintain data on a wide variety of mental health issues. These data are typically available for statistical analysis, although it often requires designing a study, asking for permission to use the data, signing a human subject's agreement to ensure data confidentiality, and sometimes paying for the use of the data. Information about many of these data sources are available on the Internet at sites such as the one maintained by Partners in Information Access for the Public Health Workforce (http://phpartners.org/health_stats.html) or the Substance Abuse and Mental Health Data Archive (http://www.icpsr.umich.edu/icpsr-web/SAMHDA/). These are sometimes complex data sets and usually require knowledge of statistics and econometrics to effectively utilize the data. If advanced statistical modeling is beyond your expertise, another approach is to review the existing literature and evidence on this issue. It is likely that you are not the first person to view this as a problem or generate data about it.

Step 2: Develop Objectives

Now that you have identified a public problem and established that it is important, you must decide on your objectives. Exactly what are you trying to accomplish? Let's say that you have decided to establish a goal of reducing by half (or some other percentage) the use of marijuana by middle school students over some specified time period. The exact percentage and length of the time period selected are, of course, debatable and critically important. Once these specifics are established, the practical question of what can we accomplish raises its head.

To be more specific, let's say you want to reduce by 50% the use of marijuana by middle school students in Bloomington, Indiana, within 2 years.

Of course, you could have chosen the State of Indiana, the Midwest, or the United States as a whole. And, once more, the time frame and percentage reduction in drug use could have been different. Your objectives will also be influenced by the resources available for this project. Moral suasion might be used at low or zero costs with law enforcement, but new programming, drug searches, or new curriculum all entail expense, and amount and sources of funding are critically important.

Step 3: Construct the Alternative Courses of Action

Even this geographically limited example is interesting because it gives rise to a large number of possible alternative courses of action, many of which are not mutually exclusive. For the sake of brevity, consider five alternative courses of action:

1. Establish an education program for parents to help them identify drug use by their children. Include reduced cost home drug tests. This is a nonpunitive approach that uses public resources and directly involves parents in this effort.

2. Require a curriculum about the dangers of drug use, potential adverse health consequences, and likely legal ramifications if caught violating the law. Provide strategies to "say no" to peer pressure and drug sellers. This approach directly targets children.

3. Increase legal sanctions for individuals selling drugs within a specified proximity to middle schools as well as sanctions for selling drugs to children. This is a strictly legal enforcement approach to the problem.

4. Increase the sanctions for using drugs for middle school children. This could be done either by families (e.g., contracts spelling out consequences for drug use), within schools (e.g., suspensions, expulsions, and detentions), or by the law (e.g., mandatory drug classes, incarceration).

5. Institute random locker checks and bring in dogs trained to sniff out drugs at the entrances to the middle schools. This could be done by law enforcement or schools.

Obviously, there are many other possibilities. To obtain a full range of options, you may want to conduct a review of best practices on drug prevention for this age-group, convene a town hall meeting to flesh out options, set up a series of focus groups of key stakeholders (e.g., students, parents, law enforcement officials, teachers, and counselors). Get the viable possibilities on the table.

Step 4: Evaluate the Alternative Courses of Action _____

Evaluating the alternative policy options is the soul of policy analysis. Let's think about drug use among middle school students as a national problem. A policy analyst would review the existing evidence about the viable alternative courses of action and would recommend any one or some subset of the following:

- *A randomized multisite national experiment to determine the impacts of each approach on drug use by middle school children.* Study sites would be selected and treatments would be randomly assigned to prospective participants. For example, students in some middle schools would be assigned to the education program whereas others would not. Alternatively, only some parents would be randomly selected for the parental education program. This approach generally works well with education programs but is less likely to work with legal sanctions. For the sake of fairness, some citizens are not systematically subjected to stricter sanctions than others for the same offense. While random assignment studies are considered the "gold standard" in evaluation, they require time, considerable expertise, and expense. However, if the case was made that this is a sufficiently important public problem, this approach would be perfectly reasonable. A good example of this type of study was done on the impacts of abstinence-only sex education (see Trenholm et al., 2008).
- *A demonstration program.* Let's say that you have designed a program that you want to implement, but that random assignment is not feasible. Perhaps it has to do with equity and fairness considerations related to legal sanctions, or perhaps you cannot amass the resources for a large-scale randomized experiment. In this case, you can implement the program in one or two sites and track the progress of participants. If you want to do this, you will essentially be conducting a quasi-experiment and you need to establish a counterfactual. How would the participants have fared in the absence of the program or policy? In other words, you will need a group of similar individuals who are not participating in the program or who are not subject to the new local law or policy to obtain a reasonable estimate of the impact of the law.
- *Stricter enforcement and sanctions.* Depending on how many sites participate in the new enforcement or sanctions, the analyst may want to conduct an interrupted time-series design or a panel study. In the case of the interrupted time series, the outcomes prior to the new laws serve as the counterfactual. In a panel study, multiple sites are tracked over time, some with the new laws and others without. This works well if the laws can be phased in or staggered.
- You may not have the skills of a policy analyst and may not be able to implement an evaluation, experiment, cost–benefit assessment, or use

any of the other methods generally taught to policy analysts. In this case, you can search for information on best practices. Use the Internet and personal and professional networks to assess what has been done already and how it appears to have worked. If you can find a meta-analysis related to your desired outcome (e.g., reduce drug use), then you are in a good situation. Meta-analyses will capitalize on the differences in sites, data sources, and methodologies to provide a broader assessment of the impact of particular programs.

Step 5: Choose the Course of Action

If you can assess the alternative courses of actions and project their likely outcomes, then you are lucky if one alternative dominates the other. That is, if one alternative maximizes the benefits for all groups and minimizes the costs for all groups, it will be the preferred choice. This, however, is seldom the case. One alternative may impose costs disproportionately on one group such as the parents, whereas others may impose higher costs on teachers or law enforcement officials or students. Essentially, in making a choice between alternatives, you are trading-off benefits and costs across different individuals and groups in our society. While this is inevitable, you need to be aware of these trade-offs and be prepared to justify your choices. Sometimes, this justification is financial. At other times, the considerations are expediency, fairness, equity, social justice, or some other factor.

Once we have chosen our preferred course of action and understand how we can justify it, we are ready to develop a consensus, build a coalition, reach an agreement, and attempt to implement the program. Even though it looks like a solid alternative, many excellent programs and policies have been nixed by political or economic considerations. This is no reason to give up, but it may require a trip back to an earlier step of policy analysis: redefining the problem or rethinking the alternatives.

Note that these steps do not end when we change our public policies. This simply establishes a new baseline from which to evaluate new improvements or changes. In some cases, new policies create unintended side effects, which we call externalities, that can be either positive or negative. Policy analysts will want to take these externalities into account when reconsidering future policy decisions.

Chapter 2 details the rationales for public sector intervention. Chapter 3 describes how a variety of mental health issues are actually addressed by public policies. Chapter 4 provides case studies and discussion questions that are useful for instructors. Chapter 5 concludes the book by focusing on *how* public policies change and provides advice for mental health advocates.

2 Rationales for Public Sector Interventions

The idealized, perfectly competitive market leads to an allocation of goods and services that is Pareto optimal—that is, you cannot make one person better off without making someone else worse off. From a societal perspective, we would not want a Pareto inferior distribution—one in which we could make someone better off without making anyone else worse off. So when markets are operating perfectly, the utility maximizing behavior of consumers and the profit maximizing behaviors of firms will, via the invisible hand, lead to Pareto optimality.

But markets do not operate perfectly all of the time. Hence, one rationale for public intervention is that some assumptions of the perfectly competitive market do not always hold and can give rise to *market failures*. Public goods, externalities, natural monopolies, and information asymmetries are four recognized market failures. As elaborated in far more detail in Weimer and Vining (2011), each of these will be described briefly in this chapter with examples from the field of mental health. Other assumptions of the competitive market can also fail to be met in practice. For example, the model of perfect competition assumes that individuals act competitively and their preferences are rational, exogenous, and fixed. When these assumptions fail to hold, the public sector can intervene. However, distributional equity, economic opportunity, protection of human rights, and civic engagement are also important considerations of governments. Societies can choose to sacrifice some market efficiency to secure a fairer distribution, protect basic human rights or dignity, or achieve a more reasonable distribution of income, wealth, goods, or services.

Market Failures

Private goods are distinguished from *public* goods by two key characteristics: Public goods are *nonexcludable* in use and *nonrivalrous* in consumption. To varying extents, private goods do not share one or both of these characteristics. Excludable ownership means that the individual has control over the use of the good. If you own a car, for example, nobody else can drive it whether you are driving it or not, you can decide about whether or not you are willing to lend it out and, if so, to whom. A good is nonrivalrous in consumption if more than one person can enjoy the benefits of the good at the same time. A common example of a good that is nonrivalrous is safe streets. A new member of a community with safe streets can enjoy the safety of the community without diminishing the utility of other residents. One additional factor to consider is *crowding*. Crowding refers to the fact that some goods may be nonrivalrous over a range of use. For example, normal usage of a suicide hotline is nonrivalrous with normal or anticipated demand levels. However, if there is a rash of suicidal ideations and calls to the hotline, then one person's use of the service may, in fact, exclude someone else from using the service. The same would be true of calls to 911, the fire department, or any other emergency responders.

In many respects, knowledge or information is a public good unless the intellectual property is owned by a corporation. But public knowledge is both nonexcludable and nonrivalrous. Adding to the public's stock of knowledge can accelerate innovation. This is one reason why governments are directly involved in the production of information. For example, in 1946, President Harry Truman signed the National Mental Health Act forming the National Institute of Mental Health (NIMH), which came into being by 1949. The NIMH is an agency of the U.S. Department of Health and Human Services and has primary responsibility for biomedical and health research. Its mission is to "transform the understanding and treatment of mental illnesses through basic and clinical research, paving the way for prevention, recovery, and cure." Its annual budget exceeds $1.5 billion, and it is arguably the largest mental health organization globally (NIMH, 2011). Research funded by the NIMH is in the public domain. It is both nonrivalrous and nonexcludable. Unlike the work of private firms, the intellectual property rights are shared for all interested parties. In the absence of government intervention, this type of knowledge would be undersupplied (as with national defense or any other public good).

An *externality* (or transaction spillover) refers to any cost or benefit resulting from any activity that affects someone who did not fully consent to the action. When externalities exist, prices in the competitive market will not reflect the full costs or benefits of producing or consuming a good or service. For example, smoking cigarettes imposes secondhand smoke and all associated health risks on individuals near the smoker, raising both ethical and political issues. Effective treatments for drug addicts not only benefit the addicts themselves but also have additional benefits for their friends, family members, and members of their local communities. The failure of the market to reflect the full costs or benefits of production or consumption provides another rationale for government intervention.

The term *monopoly* refers to markets in which there is a single seller of a product or service regardless of whether the market is local, regional, national, or even larger. The term *natural monopoly* refers to the situation where the average cost of production declines over the relevant range of demand, meaning that this market structure produces the good or service at the lowest average cost. Before cell phones and the divesture of American Telephone and Telegraph (AT&T), phone services were considered a natural monopoly. It would have been prohibitively expensive for another company to duplicate all of AT&T's phone lines, and the cost of extending service to one more user was much less expensive for AT&T than any other potential new service provider. But the prices of services are higher and quantities delivered lower when there are natural monopolies. Hence, one of the problems of natural monopolies is that of undersupply. Additionally, natural monopolies may not produce at their minimum cost, and this inefficiency, termed X-inefficiency, is one more reason for government regulation and intervention in such markets. This is why we see more government regulation of utilities, cable services, and phone services and why the government is interested in preventing corporate mergers that essentially create monopolies.

In terms of health and mental health, natural monopolies are most likely to be found in small towns and cities where it would not make sense to have two or more hospitals, mental health facilities, or surgery centers. The cost of the infrastructure and medical equipment is substantial in these facilities and one service provider can offer services at lower average costs than two or more. However, as you look beyond the small town, there are many alternatives to noncritical care. Competition and the invisible hand are not far away, and citizens will exercise their preferences based on quality of care, price, and convenience.

When we think about *information asymmetries*, we think about situations in which the amount of information about a good or service varies in relevant ways across persons. Sellers of medical procedures, mental health treatments, drugs, and used cars may be aware of potential adverse consequences of services or goods under consideration that are not immediately evident to prospective buyers. Hence, there is an imbalance in information between the sellers, or externality generators, and buyers, or affected parties. When pondering information asymmetries, we seldom think about pens, sofas, or other goods whose characteristics can be determined prior to making a purchase. These types of goods are coined search goods. Their properties can be largely ascertained before you purchase the good. Experience goods, on the other hand, are goods whose properties cannot be ascertained until they are actually purchased. Examples of experience goods include many simple medical procedures, spa services, and music concerts. Postexperience goods are those goods and services that are difficult for consumers to evaluate even after they have begun consuming them. It may be unclear if new health problems are a negative consequence of a new antidepressant drug you are taking or other mental health treatments or are related to something else. The effects of counseling may not be fully appreciated for months or even years. The effects of brain surgeries for mental health disorders such as severe obsessive compulsive disorder are not known until after the surgery (Carey, 2009).

There is a role for government intervention when information asymmetries are serious, as is the case with many postexperience goods and services. Hence, we have federal and state lemon laws for transportation vehicles and other consumer products such as computers and household appliances. (For an example, go to http://www.carlemon.com/lemons.html.) Also, there are strict regulations of drugs by the U.S. Food and Drug Administration (FDA) as well as strict monitoring and reporting requirements for all experimental medical treatments.

The idealized competitive market assumes that individuals have a set of *preferences that are rational, unchanging, and exogenously determined.* If advertising changes preferences (not for brands but for total quantity consumed), then it leads to inefficiencies in the market place. Many drugs are now directly marketed to the public, elaborating the symptoms they are supposed to benefit. Also, if consumption of addictive goods like alcohol, drugs, or tobacco actually changes preferences, requiring increasing consumption for satisfaction, then the assumption of fixed preferences is violated as well as the assumption that preferences are rational and exogenously determined. In such cases, information asymmetries concerning the future health consequences of consumption can lead to over consumption, and there is a role for government intervention. The U.S. FDA regulates what pharmaceutical companies can claim about the effectiveness of their products.

Another example when preferences may not be rational and the public sector intervenes is when individuals have serious mental illnesses and are dangerous to themselves or others or are gravely disabled. When any of these legal definitions are met, an individual can be involuntarily committed to mental health treatment. In Indiana, for example, there are four types of involuntary commitment: immediate detention (24 hours requiring a law enforcement official's signature); emergency detention (72 hours requiring a doctor's and a judge's signatures); temporary commitment (90 days mandated in- or outpatient treatment requiring a judge's commitment order); and regular commitment (annual, renewable in- or outpatient treatment requiring a judge's commitment order). Involuntary commitment violates the normal civil liberties of individuals, and the government intervenes via the courts because mentally ill individuals may not possess rational preferences. They may also pose a risk of imposing negative externalities (harm to others), if left on their own. In other cases, this type of detention may also help preserve safety and the basic human dignity of the affected party.

Many individuals donate to charities because they care about the well-being of others and derive utility from these donations in addition to the utility derived from their own personal consumption. In general, this behavior is Pareto improving, unless others care about the relative distribution of goods or wealth. This might occur, for example, if your colleague gets a raise or bonus and you do not. Even though your consumption is not diminished, you feel worse off because your consumption relative to that of your colleague has declined. If you need to *"keep up with the Joneses,"* then distributional changes become important in ways that are difficult to interpret for the Pareto principle. This type of behavior is unlikely to lead to serious market inefficiencies in the mental health arena unless people want the same prescriptions or treatments as their acquaintances for particular illnesses. While this behavior obviously can occur, physicians are gate keepers and must still prescribe medications, although they may not be insensitive to the desires of patients to try new treatments. Perhaps more relevant in this regards are the plethora of new health centers and clinics that replicate the exceptionally expensive imaging and diagnostic equipment of one another because they want to be a full-service facility and not outdone by local competitors. This type of behavior raises health care costs, a target of the 2010 Affordable Care Act.

Governments *redistribute* wealth: from the working-age population to the elderly; from middle- and upper-income families to low-income families; from smokers and drinkers to nonsmokers and nondrinkers (via taxes on cigarettes and liquor) and vice versa (through public payment for medical treatments for alcoholism and the many adverse consequences of smoking); from drivers owning vehicles to public transit riders; from the public-at-large to the hungry, ill, victims of natural disasters, students in state-subsidized colleges, and so on. Most citizens would concur that it is important to keep other citizens from starving, help out in times of disasters, or discourage behaviors like drinking and smoking that impose negative externalities on the public (through secondhand smoke, drunk driving fatalities, and uninsured medical costs).

Another way in which we redistribute income is through our public hospitals and health systems. Public hospitals are considered safety net hospitals that provide care to the uninsured and underinsured as well as others. The National Association of Public Hospitals and Health Systems (2011) indicated that their members rely on government funding sources for more than two thirds of their revenue—Medicaid (35%), Medicare (21%), and state and local governments (12%). The role of government in health care has been more hotly debated in the United States than in other developed countries, virtually all possessing some form of universal health care coverage. Government took on a much larger role in health care with the March 23, 2010, enactment of the Affordable Care Act.

When it comes to redistribution, the issue is not whether the government should be involved, but the extent of the involvement. Ultimately, the scope of tax and transfer schemes is decided by the voters in a democracy, and there is considerable variability across developed democracies as to the level of inequality in society that is acceptable.

_____**Summary**

The rationales for government intervention in the market described here are those that bear the most relevance to mental health and health care markets. The knowledge generated by NIMH and their grantees are *public goods*. They are *nonexcludable* in use and *nonrivalrous* in consumption. Addicts do not bear the full cost of their consumption. These costs, termed *negative externalities*, are also borne by parents, friends, and community members and can include drunk driving fatalities, suicides, and crime. The market inefficiency resulting from these negative externalities is another reason for collective action. *Natural monopolies* are not likely to present serious problems in mental health care except perhaps in small towns where there may be limited choice among local service providers. Information asymmetries exist for *experience* and *postexperience* goods or services— goods and services whose full set of attributes cannot be ascertained until the product or service is consumed or even afterward. This *information asymmetry* provides another rationale for government intervention. One of the assumptions of the perfectly competitive market is that *preferences are rational, exogenous, and fixed*. There are many circumstances when these assumptions do not hold. Peer pressure, addictive cravings, or serious mental disorders are all examples that violate this assumption and, consequently, can necessitate government intervention. *Altruism* generally is Pareto improving, but if individuals compare themselves with others and feel the need to *keep up with the Joneses*, this will also lead to costly market distortions that can require government intervention. Finally, *equity and fairness* considerations necessitate the *redistribution* of wealth in societies. How much wealth is redistributed varies a great deal from country to country and even from one local geographic area to another—reflecting different beliefs and preferences about equality, poverty, and fairness.

3 How Prevention Efforts Are Addressed by Public Policies

Public policy addresses mental health in critically important ways. To mention a few, we have drugs approved by the FDA, Medicare/Medicaid and state children's health insurance programs, state laws related to governing suicide prevention and assisted suicides, court determinations on mental competency and commitments, and laws related to substances of abuse (tobacco, alcohol, and illicit drugs). State and local mental hospitals are other obvious and sometimes ominous specters of public policy.

The ways in which public policy and mental health intersect is sometimes a complex matter. Often public policies have preventative qualities that may not have been their primary directive. For example, Brown and Susser (2008) found that one of the risk factors for the development of schizophrenia is inadequate nutrition in utero. The nutritional program Women, Infants, and Children (WIC) reduces this risk factor by providing nutrition to individuals who may not be able to access adequate nutritional resources independently. Historically, legislation has addressed mental health in a very general way. But increasingly, public policies are being developed with the intention of targeting specific mental disorders. The Federal Response to Eliminate Eating Disorders Act (FREED), introduced on March 3, 2011, is one such example.

To implement a public policy to prevent a mental disorder, it is important to first understand what is being prevented. Mental health professionals have worked together to achieve a consensus on the symptoms of mental disorders. The *Diagnostic and Statistical Manual of Mental Disorders*, fourth edition, text revision (*DSM-IV-TR*; American Psychiatric Association [APA], 2000), contains the current standards used in practice today. The *DSM-IV-TR* conceptualizes mental disorders as a "clinically significant behavioral of psychological syndrome or pattern that occurs in an individual and that is associated with present distress or disability or with a significantly increased risk of suffering death, pain, disability or an important loss of freedom" (p. xxxi). It is important to note that this text is currently undergoing revision and is anticipated to be rereleased in 2013.

Another integral part of preventing mental disorders is having an understanding of how they develop. Developmental psychopathology theorizes that the development of mental disorders occurs in the same way as other more normative behaviors (Broderick & Blewitt, 2010). Each individual has strengths and vulnerabilities that contribute to a particular outcome. An individual's vulnerabilities, or risk factors, can interfere with healthy development. An individual's strengths, or protective factors, help promote healthy outcomes. These factors can be biological, environmental, or both. How the interaction between an individual's genes and environment results in a particular disorder is complex and is not yet fully understood.

Prevention is not an exact science. There is no definite way that one can determine if an individual will develop a particular disorder. Thus, it is important to be able to examine the risk and protective factors associated with the disorder in question. Some risk factors can be eliminated, others can be moderated, and others are permanent. Prevention interventions focus on the risk factors that can be eliminated and moderated. Let's continue with the example of schizophrenia. The strongest predictor of the development of schizophrenia is a familial history of the disorder (Mortensen, Pedersen, & Pedersen, 2010). This represents a risk factor that cannot, with our current technology, be altered. Suvisaari (2010) found that genetically susceptible children are more vulnerable to the effects of an unstable child rearing environment. This risk factor can be moderated by providing parents with a familial history of schizophrenia with parenting classes and by increasing their support networks. Substance use, another risk factor (Harley et al., 2010), can be eliminated by abstaining from the use of drugs and alcohol.

Prevention interventions often seek to increase protective factors as well as reduce risk factors to moderate an individual's likelihood of developing particular disorders. Similar to risk factors, some can be changed and others cannot. For example, one of the protective factors for the development of substance use disorders is an easy temperament (Arthur, Hawkins, Pollard, Catalano, & Baglioni, 2002). While temperament can be influenced by the environments in which children are raised, government ability to manipulate home environments is limited.

This chapter will discuss the importance of screening for mental disorders and their risk factors. Next, three different psychological phenomenon will be discussed; they are substance use disorders, depression, and suicide. Within each of these areas several subjects will be discussed including their *DSM-IV-TR* definition (when appropriate), their risk and protective factors, and the policy related to the prevention of these phenomena. The focus will be primarily on federal and state legislation and policies, as these affect the largest number of individuals. However, it is important to understand that policies can be implemented on a very wide scale, ranging from federal to policies that affect a county, city, and a single individual.

General Screening

The use of screening is critical in the prevention of mental disorders. Screening enables populations at the greatest risk for specific disorders to be targeted with interventions. It is important to ensure that interventions are both cost-effective and effective therapeutically. Interestingly, it has been noted that for certain interventions aimed at reducing criminal recidivism (Andrews et al., 1990), providing treatment to high- and low-risk populations (failure to screen) is counterproductive and increases recidivism probabilities for low-risk individuals.

The Importance of School Counseling

A good deal of attention is paid to mental health screening and prevention in schools. Half of all lifetime instances of mental disorders occur prior to the age of 14 years (Kessler et al., 2005). Additionally, children often present with risk factors and display warning signs prior to the development of mental disorders. Thus, schools can serve as a venue for the primary prevention of many disorders. Schools are also logical venues for prevention programs because children spend large portions of their days at school. Teachers spend more time with children than any other adult figure, except perhaps for parents. Therefore, teachers can often observe signs of possible disorders as they emerge. When this occurs, it is critically important that teachers consult with school counselors.

School counselors receive special training to address mental health disorders. The American School Counselor Association (ASCA) notes that in most public school systems, school counselors are required to take course work in several core areas before they can be licensed. Some of these areas are human growth and development as well as research and program evaluation (ASCA, 2010). If the school counselor was not trained at a program accredited by the Council for Accreditation of Counseling and Related Educational Programs (CACREP, 2009), the major accrediting body, they would be required to receive training in those areas as well as assessment. This background qualifies school counselors to identify risk factors for mental diseases and implement appropriate prevention programs to ameliorate some of the presenting risk factors and strengthen the protective factors.

School counselor education is important in other ways. For example, the Improving America's School Act of 1994, an amendment to the Elementary and Secondary Education Act, requires that school counselors attend a CACREP-accredited program to receive federal monies. In addition to federal policies related to school counselors, each state has its own legislation. Currently, 28 states and the District of Columbia mandate that counselors be employed at all grade levels (ASCA, 2010). For an up-to-date listing and detailed description of each state's laws, visit the ASCA's website: http://www.schoolcounselor.org.

The Importance of Mental Health Courts

While there are several forms of screening targeted at youth, very few exist for adults. One area where screening for adults does occur is within the legal system. Individuals with mental disorders are more likely to be arrested. Studies show that these individuals constitute 6% of the general population, but 10% to 15% of the jail and prison population (Lamb & Weinberber, 1998). One intervention that has been used to target this issue is the use of mental health courts.

Mental health courts provide alternatives to incarceration for individuals with mental disorders. These courts coordinate with community mental health centers to provide individuals with evidence-based interventions. Evaluations of these programs have shown reductions in recidivism (Hiday & Ray, 2010), suggesting that this tertiary form of prevention is effective.

Mental health courts are a recent phenomenon. The first mental health court was established in Indianapolis, Indiana, in 1996. Currently, more than 250 mental health courts are in existence with many more being established (Morrissey, Fagan, & Cocozza, 2009). These programs are supported under the America's Law Enforcement and Mental Health Project and Mentally Ill Offender Treatment and Crime Reduction Act of 2004.

_____ Policies Targeting Psychological Phenomena

Federal policies related to mental disorder prevention began in 1946 with the passing of the National Mental Health Act. This legislation provided the funding for research, training of professional personnel, and funding for states to establish pilot and demonstration projects. It resulted in the establishment of the NIMH in 1949. This organization has a significant impact on the development of mental health policies in the United States.

Substance-Related Disorders

Most young people who try substances (tobacco, alcohol, and other drugs) will not go on to develop problems with abuse or dependence (Thombs, 2006). As noted earlier, distinguishing individuals who develop disorders from those who do not is central to prevention. There are several risk and protective factors associated with the development of these types of disorders. These factors occur on many different levels ranging from the community to the individual. Often legislation targets larger community factors. Some of the community risk factors are laws or norms that are favorable to drug use, media portrayals of alcohol use, low neighborhood attachment, and extreme economic deprivation. Some of the protective factors, which programs often attempt to increase, are opportunities for prosocial involvement, recognition for positive involvement, bonding, and healthy beliefs and standards for behavior (Catalano, Haggerty, Hawkins, & Elgin, 2011). Prevention programs, which are often funded through federal and state legislation, often target the more local aspects such as family, school, and individual factors. For a more detailed description of substance use risk and protective factors, see Catalano et al. (2011).

Substance use prevention legislation has one of the most obvious connections between the disorder it intends to prevent, its risk factors, and the law. The *DSM-IV-TR* defines substance dependence as a maladaptive pattern of substance use, leading to clinically significant impairment or distress (APA, 2000, p. 197). While there is a general diagnostic criterion for substance dependence, the *DSM-IV-TR* defines the criteria for dependence on different substances, including nicotine, alcohol, and illegal drugs. This is important, as some substances differ slightly in their diagnostic criteria. For example, individuals will not typically spend a great deal of time trying to obtain nicotine because it is legal and readily available (APA, 2000).

Nicotine Use, Abuse, and Dependence

Prevention efforts regarding tobacco have been widespread and prominent in the media. It is safe to say that most Americans know that tobacco use is dangerous. The 1964 Surgeon General Report linked cigarette smoking to lung cancer and other respiratory illnesses. Smoking rates are declining in the United States. This leaves tobacco corporations scrambling for customers. Studies show that individuals who don't smoke before the age of 21 years are likely to remain nonsmokers (American Council for Drug Education [ACDE], 1999). As a result, tobacco corporations target children.

Master Settlement Agreement. The government took note of this and in 1998 arranged an agreement between 4 prominent tobacco corporations and 46 states, called the Master Settlement Agreement (MSA). The tobacco corporations agreed to pay $206 billion over a 25-year period and follow regulations about advertisement and distribution of tobacco products. In exchange, the participating states settled their unresolved Medicaid claims against those tobacco corporations. Texas, Florida, Minnesota, and Mississippi settled separately. Annually, this money is divided among the participating states to cover tobacco-related health expenditures, and a portion is given to an antismoking foundation.

Each state dictates how they appropriate these funds. In concordance with the agreement, this money was to be allocated toward smoking prevention and smoking cessation programs, in addition to other tobacco-related public health issues. One of the ways in which many states use portions of this funding is for quit lines. More than one third of the state quit lines provide free cessation medications to qualified callers (Cummins, Bailey, Campbell, Koon-Kirby, & Zhu, 2007). One study found that individuals who use some form of nicotine replacement were 1.5 to 2 times more likely to quit than individuals who did not use any form of nicotine replacement (Silagy, Lancaster, Stead, Mant, & Fowler, 2004).

One of the major goals of the MSA was to eliminate the advertising that targeted youth. Statistics show that the average age of first tobacco use is 13 years (ACDE, 1999). Tobacco corporations participating in the MSA cannot use advertising that targets youth. A portion of the MSA explicitly states that cartoons cannot be used in advertising. One study showed that after Joe Camel was introduced in 1988, adolescent cigarette use rose from less than 1% in 1988 to 8% in 1989, to more than 13% in 1993 (U.S. Department of Health and Human Services [USDHHS], Office of the Surgeon General, 2000). Additional MSA restrictions on advertising include elimination of outdoor and transit advertising and elimination of product placement in the media.

The MSA also restricts the way in which tobacco can be distributed. Participating tobacco corporations are not permitted to distribute cigarettes in packs of less than 20. These smaller packs have been termed *kiddy packs* as they tend to be largely consumed by adolescents. The participating tobacco corporations are also restricted from giving free samples or merchandise to individuals who are underage.

The final portion of the MSA allocates money toward "the foundation." The purpose of the foundation is to educate youth about tobacco, substance abuse, and related health problems. Studies have shown that youth-targeted antismoking campaigns, such as the Truth, can have attitudinal and behavioral changes (e.g., Richardson, Green, Xiao, Sokol, & Vallone, 2010). The foundation is also responsible for grant writing for research in youth tobacco use, establishment of effective prevention programs, and disseminating educational information in the media, in classrooms, and through other related programs.

Family Smoking Prevention and Control Act. This Act (Tobacco Control Act) was signed into legislation on June 22, 2009, by President Barack Obama. This landmark legislation was formed in response to the *FDA v. Brown & Williamson Tobacco Corp*. It gives the FDA the authority to regulate the manufacture, marketing, and retail of tobacco products, which was not previously covered under the Federal Food, Drugs and Cosmetics Act.

In addition to affording the FDA the right to regulate tobacco, the Tobacco Control Act had several other provisions. It mandated that the terms *mild*, *low*, and *light* no longer be utilized because they misrepresented the risk of smoking cigarettes. This is because smokers mistakenly believe that these cigarettes cause fewer health problems.

Additionally, tobacco companies must now place warning labels on cigarette packs that cover 50% of the front and back of the package. As discussed earlier, policies can have different levels of prevention depending on the population to which they are applied. For individuals who are nonsmokers, this acts as a form of primary prevention. However, for smokers this acts as a form of tertiary prevention.

As a part of the Tobacco Control Act Congress banned the sale of flavored cigarettes (other than menthol). This was done because flavored cigarettes were targeting youth. In 2004, research showed that smokers who were 17 years old were three times as likely to smoke flavored cigarettes as smokers over the age of 20 (Klein et al., 2008). In addition, these individuals viewed flavored tobacco products as safer than nonflavored cigarettes (Primack et al., 2008).

Another example of primary prevention under the Tobacco Control Act is the FDAs Regulations Restricting the Sale and Distribution of Cigarettes and Smokeless Tobacco to Protect Children and Adolescents Rule (Tobacco Rule), which was signed in on June 22, 2010. This rule regulates the sale, distribution, and marketing of cigarettes and smokeless tobacco products. This rule has multiple aspects.

One of the major focuses of this rule is to regulate how tobacco corporations sell and distribute their products. As a result of this rule, which acts as a law, sale of tobacco to individuals under the age of 18 is now federally prohibited. Prior to this rule, the minimum age to purchase tobacco products was regulated by each state. Regulations regarding the place of sale of cigarettes stipulate they not be sold in vending machines unless they are in an adults-only restricted area. Regulations regarding packaging dictate the sale of cigarettes in packages of 20 or more. Furthermore, free samples of cigarettes and smokeless tobacco are prohibited.

The other major focus of this legislation is on marketing. In the 2000 Surgeon General's Report on Reducing Tobacco Use, it was reported that by regulating advertising it is likely to reduce the initiation of smoking (USDHHS, Office of the Surgeon General, 2000). Tobacco companies are no longer allowed to sponsor athletic, musical, or other social or cultural events. They are prohibited from giving gifts in exchange for purchasing cigarettes. They are further prohibited from distributing products that have their logos. Finally, audio advertisement is restricted to words only. For a more detailed description of the Tobacco Rule, visit the FDA's website http://www.fda.gov.

Two additional provisions of the Tobacco Rule have yet to be signed into law due to legal concerns. The FDA attempted to restrict the advertising of tobacco products within 1,000 ft. of a school or playground. This provision has not become law yet because it allegedly violates First Amendment rights. The second provision that has been delayed is also related to First Amendment rights. The legislation attempts to prohibit tobacco-related advertising in magazines, where the youth readership is greater than 15% or 2 million youth for each magazine.

There is a history of federal legislation restricting tobacco advertising. The Public Health Cigarette Smoking Act of 1969 banned television and radio advertising of cigarettes. More advertising restrictions were passed in 1984 with the Comprehensive Smokeless Tobacco Health Education Act, which banned smokeless tobacco advertising from any broadcast media.

Taxation. Taxation acts as a form of primary prevention for nontobacco users and as a form of tertiary prevention for tobacco users. By increasing the cost of cigarettes, taxes restrict access. There are currently both federal and state taxes on cigarettes. On April 1, 2009, a tax hike on cigarettes raised the tax from 39 cents to $1.01 per pack, making it the largest tax hike on cigarettes ever in the United States. In a statement issued by Charles D. Conner (2009), the president and Chief Executive Officer of the American Lung Association (ALA), it was reported that for every 10% increase in the cost of cigarettes there is a 7% reduction in youth smoking.

Restriction of Access. Another prominent form of tertiary prevention related to cigarettes in the United States is the restriction of where an individual can smoke. There is federal legislation prohibiting smoking on airplanes, in federal government buildings, in libraries, in prisons and jails, on public transportation, and in day care facilities and schools that serve individuals under the age of 18 and also receive federal funds. By reducing the number of places individuals can smoke, this acts as a form of primary prevention for nonsmokers, especially children, because it reduces the number of smoking models.

Each state also has laws regulating where individuals can and cannot smoke. Each has its own strengths and limitations. Clean Indoor Air laws generally pertain to state/local government buildings, private workplaces, restaurants, and bars. Presented here is a map of grades the ALA has attributed to the legislation each state has on clean air laws. The grades are as follows: A, B, C, D, F.

Figure 3.1   Clean Air Law Grades Assigned by the American Lung Association

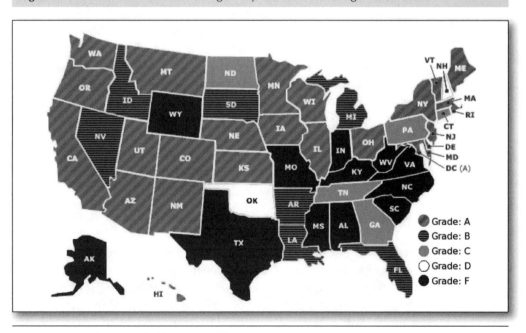

Source: American Lung Association [ALA], 2010.

California, Maine, Arkansas, and Louisiana have taken their clean air laws a step further and have regulated when individuals can smoke with children in the car. For example, California has a law that prohibits individuals from smoking with children younger than 18 years of age present. Maine restricts smoking in a vehicle with children younger than the age of 16 present. Indiana, Maine, New Jersey, Oregon, Pennsylvania, Texas, Vermont, and Washington have legislation that restricts individuals from smoking in a vehicle with a foster child present. Texas, Vermont, and Washington restrict foster parents from smoking in their homes when children are present.

Inspection of Retailers. One of the ways in which each state government prevents nicotine addiction is to inspect retailers to determine that they are complying with the state and federal laws regarding the minimum age to purchase. As mentioned earlier, the Tobacco Control Act established a minimum age of 18 to purchase tobacco in the United States. However, prior to this act, the minimum age to purchase was regulated by each state and local government. Each state has a governing body that performs surprise inspections of retailers that distribute tobacco products. Hefty fines are given to retailers that do not comply.

State Laws. Each state is required to follow federal laws regarding tobacco regulation. They also institute their own laws regarding tobacco. A detailed description of each state's tobacco legislation is given at the State Legislated Actions on Tobacco Issues website: http://www.lungusa2.org/slati/.

Local/Company Policies. Local policies are largely out of the scope of this book. However, it is important to note the impact that local and company policies can have on a large number of individuals. Take Universal Pictures' policy regarding tobacco depiction in films. They aim to reduce the incidence of tobacco use in their films targeted at youth. The only instances where smoking will be depicted in their films are when it is considered significantly important. In such instances, there will be a warning against smoking in the credits as well as on the packaging of the DVD. Universal Studios also refuses to place products for tobacco companies in films, regardless of a film's rating (Universal Pictures, 2007). This is important as community norms that favor cigarette use are significant risk factors for the later development of tobacco-related problems (Beyers, Toumbourou, Catalano, Arthur, & Hawkins, 2004).

Alcohol Use, Abuse, and Dependence

Media and researchers have paid considerable attention to alcohol use disorders. Alcohol, tobacco, and marijuana are the substances most frequently abused by adolescents (Latimer & Zur, 2010). The use of alcohol in adolescence predicts higher rates of problem drinking as an adult (Rohde, Lewinsohn, Kahler, Seeley, & Brown, 2001). Interestingly, adolescent tobacco use is the strongest predictive factor of adult alcohol abuse. Furthermore, the combination of adolescent problem alcohol use and problem marijuana use is the strongest predictor of adult substance use disorders (Stenbacka, 2003).

National Minimum Drinking Age Act of 1984. Risk factors for substance abuse disorders such as parental substance use are strongly correlated with the age at which adolescents initiate substance use. One study found that the younger an individual when initiating alcohol use, the greater his or her later problems with alcohol misuse (Hawkins et al., 1997). The National Minimum Drinking Age Act of 1984 thus serves as a preventative measure against the later development of alcohol use disorders.

The National Minimum Drinking Age Act states that individuals must be 21 years old to purchase and publicly possess alcohol. If individual states do not enforce this law, they run the risk of losing 10% of their annual federal highway appointment under the Federal Aid Highway Act. However, this act did not create an outright ban on the consumption of alcohol for individuals younger than 21 years. Only some states and the District of Columbia (e.g., Indiana and Kansas) have a complete ban on alcohol use and possession by individuals younger than 21 years. A majority of states (e.g., California and New York) have some type of exception to this law such as allowing minors to consume alcohol in the presence of a parent or spouse or consuming alcohol in a private residential setting. For a more detailed description of the exceptions to this legislation, visit the National Institute of Alcohol Abuse and Alcoholism's (NIAAA's) Alcohol Policy Information System at http://alcohol policy.niaaa.nih.gov/Home.html.

Fetal Alcohol Spectrum Disorders

Fetal Alcohol Spectrum Disorders (FASD) is a nonclinical term used for a range of disorders that result from maternal consumption of alcohol while pregnant. The effects include physical, mental, behavioral, and learning disabilities. Alcohol exposure at different periods of fetal development results in different cognitive and physical abnormalities (Coles, 1994; Maier, Chen, & West, 1996). FASD are believed to be the most common nonhereditary form of mental retardation (NIAAA, 2010). Fetal Alcohol Syndrome (FAS) is the most severe form of FASD. The U.S. Surgeon General warns that no amount of alcohol is considered safe during pregnancy (USDHSS, Office of the Surgeon General, 2005).

While presently there is no federal law specifically outlawing the use of alcohol while pregnant, there are several federal and state laws prohibiting child abuse. Currently 20 states have provisions pertaining to alcohol use and child neglect (NIAAA, 2010). For example, Arizona Statute s8-819 states that "in the determination of child neglect consideration will be given to . . . the use by the mother of a dangerous drug, a narcotic drug, or alcohol during pregnancy" (AZ Revised Stat. §8-819). There is currently no federal law that prohibits the use of medical tests in the prosecution of a woman who has exposed her child in utero to alcohol or other substances of abuse for the determination of child abuse. However, six states have limitations on what tests can be used in this prosecution (NIAAA, 2010).

The Sober Truth on Preventing Underage Drinking Act of 2006. The Sober Truth on Preventing Underage Drinking Act (STOP Act) authorized $18 million in federal monies to prevent underage drinking. This act targets many of the risk factors associated with the development of alcohol-related problems. The STOP Act is implemented by government and community organizations. Provisions of this act include the establishment of a committee to oversee an increase in interagency cooperation to reduce underage drinking, annual state reporting to Congress about individual efforts to eliminate underage drinking, a national media campaign aimed at adults, an assessment of the impact of media images of alcohol use on adolescents, increased resources for community coalitions increase prevention efforts, and funding for research on adolescent drinking.

Call to Action to Prevent and Reduce Underage Drinking. In March 2007, the U.S. Surgeon General issued a call to action to reduce and prevent underage drinking. A Call to Action is a scientific document intended to stimulate change in society concerning a major public health concern. They have historically been instrumental in policy change. The Call to Action to Prevent and Reduce Underage Drinking sets forth six goals to be achieved by the government, schools, parents, and society.

> GOAL 1: Foster changes in American society that facilitate healthy adolescent development and that help prevent and reduce underage drinking.

> GOAL 2: Engage parents, schools, communities, all levels of government, all social systems that interface with you, and youth themselves in a coordinated national effort to prevent and reduce drinking and its consequences.

> GOAL 3: Promote an understanding of underage alcohol consumption in the context of human development and maturation that takes into account individual adolescent characteristics as well as environmental, ethnic, cultural, and gender differences.

> GOAL 4: Conduct additional research on adolescent alcohol use and its relationship to development.

> GOAL 5: Work to improve public health surveillance on underage drinking and on population-based risk factors for this behavior.

> GOAL 6: Work to ensure that policies at all levels are consistent with the national goal of preventing and reducing underage alcohol consumption. (USDHHS, Office of the Surgeon General, 2007)

Taxation. Like tobacco, alcohol is subject to federal and state taxes, which are estimated to induce large preventative effects compared with other prevention policies (Wagenaar, Salois, & Komro, 2009). Higher taxes reduce alcohol consumption and alcohol-related harm (Elder et al., 2010).

Drug Use, Abuse, and Dependence

Prevention of substance use disorders is prominent in public policies, the media, as well as research. This trend began with the Nixon Administration's "war on drugs" in the 1970s. As noted earlier, the *DSM-IV-TR* makes a distinction between substances of abuse, distinctions also reflected in different sentencing laws for different illegal drugs. However, many public policies lump substances of abuse together, and so, this section on those government bodies, laws, and policies will focus on substances of abuse in general.

Policies aimed at attacking the drug problem in the United States are either demand- or supply-side management. Drug control efforts have traditionally focused on reducing supply (Fornili & Burda, 2010). Theoretically, a shift in supply (lower availability at all prices), causes prices to rise and the quantity demanded to fall. Increasing the penalties for drug distribution as occurred during the 1980s war on drugs should reduce the supply of drugs at all prices. The drug sentencing laws did become more punitive and led to large increases in prison populations. About 80% of prisoners have a substance use disorder (Kemp, Savitz, Thompson, & Zanis, 2004). Most do not receive treatment for their substance use disorders in prison, and two thirds return to prison within 3 years of their release (Bureau of Justice Statistics, 2011).

In the past two decades, drug courts have addressed substance abuse disorders (for a detailed discussion, see Simmons, 1999). Drug courts are alternatives to incarceration for people with substance use disorders. They incorporate substance use counseling, 12-step group attendance, drug testing, and weekly court appearances. These programs have been shown to be effective in reducing instances of addiction in participants (e.g., Dakof et al., 2010).

The Anti-Drug Abuse Act of 1986. The Anti-Drug Abuse Act of 1986, later revised in 1988, established the policy goals of a drug-free America, set mandatory sentencing minimums for drug crimes, and created the Office of the National Drug Control Policy (ONDCP). The mandatory sentencing minimums distinguish between kingpins and mid and low-level dealers based on the quantity of drugs in their possession. Under this legislation, kingpins were subject to 10-year mandatory minimums and midlevel dealers to 5-year mandatory minimums.

This legislation was considered one of the strictest laws in place regarding drug trafficking and imposes unusually hefty sentences for crack cocaine. For kingpins and midlevel dealers, the minimum quantities for crack cocaine were originally set at 1% of the minimum for powder cocaine. For example, a midlevel dealer–sentence is applicable for possessing 5 g of crack cocaine or 500 g of powder cocaine. However, in 2007, the crack cocaine sentencing guidelines were amended by the Sentencing Commission with 5 g of crack cocaine now resulting in a reduction of the mandatory minimum sentencing range from 63 to 78 months to 51 to 63 months.

The ONDCP is active in substance use prevention, an effort which is considered to be a "cost effective, common sense approach of promoting safe and healthy communities." (ONDCP, 2010, para. 1). The ONDCP's 2010 National Drug Control Strategy has five primary principles: (1) Prevention efforts should be grounded at the community level; (2) prevention efforts should occur in a range of environments where young people grow up; (3) research should be conducted to determine effective prevention efforts, and this information should be disseminated; (4) criminal justice organizations should collaborate with prevention organizations; (5) drugged driving should become a national priority equal to that of drunken driving.

The ONDCP is responsible for prevention efforts such as the Drug Free Communities (DFC) program and the National Youth Anti-Drug Media Campaign. The DFC program was funded by Congress with the understanding that local drug problems require local solutions. They provide grant money of up to $125,000 to over 700 antidrug coalitions across the country that are charged with providing local prevention efforts and disseminating information.

The National Youth Anti-Drug Media Campaign was passed by Congress in 1998 to prevent and reduce youth drug use. It distributes information about the harms of drugs through the media (e.g., cinema, television, radio, print) at the national and community levels. According to Slater, Kelley, Lawrence, Stanley, and Comello (2011), this campaign has reduced marijuana use by adolescents.

School-Targeted Legislation. School-based programs are the most prevalent form of adolescent drug prevention in use (Ringwalt, Clark, Hanley, Shamblen, & Flewelling, 2010). Unfortunately, only 10% of school districts in the United States utilize evidence-based drug prevention programs (Ringwalt et al., 2008). There is a significant amount of legislation targeting this issue, including the Safe and Drug Free Schools and Communities Act, the Safe Schools/Healthy Student (SS/HS) Initiative, and School-Based Student Drug Testing programs. There is additional legislation increasing penalties for committing drug-related crimes within a specified distance of a school.

The Safe and Drug Free Schools and Communities Act aims to reduce school violence and substance use by providing grants to fund programming. Under this act, state and local organizations are held accountable for achieving measureable results. Programs and activities must be based on objective assessments of drug use behavior, an established set of performance measures, empirically founded programs, an analysis of risk and protective factors, and include ongoing development of the program.

The SS/HS Initiative is very similar to the Safe and Drug Free Schools and Communities Act. SS/HS is a collaborative grant-writing program targeted at reducing substance use and violence among the nation's youth. It is operated by three different governmental organizations: (1) the U.S. Department of

Education, (2) the Department of Health and Human Services, and (3) the Department of Justice.

The Department of Education also funds School-Based Student Drug Testing Programs. These programs are intended to identify students with drug use problems so that they can be provided with treatment. Students enrolled in these programs must meet one of the three requirements: (1) They are enrolled in school-based athletics program; (2) they are involved in a competitive extracurricular activity; or (3) they volunteer to participate with parental agreement. These programs must conform to the state and federal laws regarding drug testing, which require confidentiality of the results.

The federal "schoolyard statute" (21 USC § 860) is a part of the Comprehensive Crime Control Act. It was adopted during the Reagan Administration to reduce the use of drugs among school-aged children (Mowery, 1997). It doubles the penalty for certain drug offenses that occur within 1,000 ft. of a school. Each state has its own individual schoolyard statute, which enables them to adopt their own regulations about what is appropriate within a certain distance from a school.

Drug Free Workplace Act of 1988. Drug use prevention programs often target youth. However, legislation such as the Drug-Free Workplace Act of 1988 targets adults as well. This legislation requires all organizations possessing a government contract of $100,000 or more and any organization receiving a federal grant to maintain a drug-free workplace. This legislation places requirements on organizations as well as its employees. Organizations are required to establish a program where employees are informed about the company's drug-free workplace policy, the penalty for violating this policy, and the availability of counseling or rehabilitation. Employees are required to notify employers of any drug-related convictions within 5 days. This legislation led to an increase in use of health benefits suggesting that an increased number of employees sought substance use–related treatment (Montoya, Carlson, & Richard, 1999).

Drug Use and Parental Rights

Environments in which substances are used put children and adolescents at risk for developing substance use disorders. Children raised in families with parents with substance use disorders are more likely to develop substance use disorders (Sawdi, 1999). Each state has adopted guidelines for what constitutes the grounds for termination of parental rights. Long-term parental drug use is one of the most common grounds for involuntary termination of rights (USDHHS, 2010). These laws vary by state. For an up-to-date description of these laws for each state, visit the U.S. Department of Health and Human Services' Child Welfare Information Gateway State Statutes at http://www.childwelfare.gov/systemwide/laws_policies/state/.

Mood-Related Disturbances

Depression

In recent years, policies have emerged to address mental disorders besides substance use. Depression is one example. Public policies related to depression usually focus on individuals rather than communities, as seen with substance use disorders. The *DSM-IV-TR* (APA, 2000) identifies three types of depressive disorders: major depressive disorder (either single episode or recurrent), dysthymic disorder, and depressive disorders not otherwise specified.

Depression is a relatively common occurrence with approximately 7% of the population experiencing depression within the last year. Rates of depression more than doubled between 1992 and 2002 (Compton, Conway, Stinson, & Grant, 2006). Risk factors for the development of major depression include being female, Native American, or middle aged or having low income (Hasin, Goodwin, Stinson, & Grant, 2005).

The majority of the existing legislation for depression focuses on postpartum depression. This is not surprising considering that postpartum depression is the most common complication of giving birth, occurring among 10% to 15% of women (Robertson, Celasun, & Stewart, 2003). There are several risk factors for the development of this disorder, including depression, anxiety, or stressful life events during pregnancy; a history of depression; low levels of social support (Robertson, Grace, Wallington, & Stewart, 2004); and fatigue (Kienhuis, Rogers, Giallo, Matthews, & Treyvaud, 2010).

Mother's Act. The Melanie Blocker Stokes Mothers Act was signed into law in March, 2010, as a part of the Patient Protection and Affordable Care Act (P.L. 111-148; Section 2952). This is the first federal legislation addressing postpartum depression. This act (a) provides grants to service providers who target women with postpartum depression or women at risk for postpartum depression; (b) requires the Secretary of Health and Human Services to conduct a study examining the benefits of screening for this disorder; (c) encourages Health and Human Services to launch a national awareness campaign; and (d) encourages Health and Human Services to coordinate and facilitate research to increase the understanding of postpartum depression.

Screening for postpartum depression is important because half of postpartum depression cases go undiagnosed (Gjerdingen & Yawn, 2007). The American Academy of Pediatrics' Committee on the Psychosocial Aspects of Child and Family Development recommends that pediatricians integrate maternal postpartum depression screening into well-child visits. Pediatricians are the medical professionals who are most likely to interact with a new mother within the first month of her child's life. However, pediatricians are not as familiar with postpartum depression screening methods as obstetricians–gynecologists (Ob/Gyn; Chadha-Hooks, Park, Hilty, & Seritan, 2010). Despite increased training in this area, only 72% of Ob/Gyn screen new mothers for this disorder (Leddy, Haaga, Gray, & Schulkin, 2011).

While federal legislation related to postpartum depression is relatively new, several states have passed legislation focused on this issue. Currently, 16 different states have either passed or have pending legislation: California (pending), Illinois (passed), Iowa (passed), Kentucky (passed), Louisiana (passed), Maine (passed), Massachusetts (pending), Minnesota (passed), New Jersey (passed), New York (pending), Oregon (passed), Pennsylvania (pending), Texas (passed), Vermont (pending), Virginia (passed), Washington (passed), and West Virginia (passed). There are also several states that have proposed legislation that did not pass, including Hawaii and New Mexico. The first state law passed was the New Jersey Postpartum Depression Law of 2006. This law requires physicians, nurse midwives, and other licensed health care professionals to screen new mothers and educate pregnant women and their families about postpartum depression.

Suicide Prevention

While suicide is not a mental disorder, it is frequently associated with mental disorders, especially depression (U.S. Public Health Services, 1999). Studies show that between 59% and 87% of individuals who commit suicide suffer from major depression (Gonda, Fountoulakis, Kaprinis, & Rihmer, 2007). In general, diagnosis of a mental disorder is a significant risk factor for suicide, with 90% of individuals who commit suicide meeting diagnostic criterion at the time of their death (Centers for Disease Control, 2007). Additional risk factors include prior suicide attempts, hopelessness, isolation, loss, and easy access to lethal means (U.S. Public Health Services, 1999). The *DSM-5* Revision Committee is considering adding assessments for suicide risk as a portion of mental health screening due to the serious nature of suicide.

Suicide prevention gained national recognition in 1997 when Congress passed resolutions recognizing suicide as a national problem. This was further supported in 1999 when the U.S. Surgeon General released a Call to Action to reduce suicide. This Call to Action recommended addressing suicide through public policy, awareness, intervention, and research. It targeted two groups for prevention efforts: youth and the elderly.

The National Strategy for Suicide Prevention, established in 2001, was developed as a result of one of the intervention recommendations of the Surgeon General's Call to Action. This document provided the scaffolding for a national suicide prevention plan. It proposed investing efforts in 11 different areas, including increasing research efforts to improve understanding and available prevention programs, reducing the stigma of receiving mental health services, and promoting efforts to reduce access to lethal means.

The National Suicide Prevention Resource Center (SPRC) was developed in reaction to the National Strategy for Suicide Prevention. It was initially funded with a $9 million federal grant in 2002. This clearinghouse provides prevention support, training, and informational services to lawmakers, service providers, and individuals. The SPRC was renamed the Garrett Lee Smith National SPRC in 2004 with the passing of the Garrett Lee Smith Memorial Act.

The Garrett Lee Smith Memorial Act. The Garrett Lee Smith Memorial Act (P.L. 108-355) was the first federal legislation to provide funding for youth suicide prevention services. This act recognizes that youth suicide is a serious problem, being the third leading cause of deaths in adolescents between the ages of 15 and 19 years (Shain & The Committee on Adolescents, 2007). It acknowledges that suicide is often related to underlying mental health issues. Eighty-two million dollars was distributed through three different types of grants over a 3-year period of time (2005–2007). The first type of grant is the SPRC grant, which funded the SPRC. The second two types of grants provided money to colleges, states, and Native American tribes to implement suicide screening and prevention interventions. Since 2007, additional funding has been provided for these programs through the Substance Abuse and Mental Health Services Administration, the organization charged with administering the funds. This legislation has gone up for reauthorization every year since 2007, but it has failed to pass each time.

Florida was the first state to pass legislation for suicide prevention with the Florida Emotional Development and Suicide Prevention Act in 1984. This law required the state to develop a youth suicide prevention plan. It led to the Comprehensive Plan for the Prevention of Youth Suicide, which proposed ways in which to foster positive emotional health and intervene when problems related to suicide arose. While the legislation was passed, it was never implemented (Florida Suicide Prevention Coalition, 2011). However, in 1990, Florida mandated that teachers should be trained in suicide prevention as a requirement of certification. To date, similar legislation has been enacted in Tennessee, New Jersey, California, Arkansas, Illinois, and Wisconsin.

U.S. Military Prevention Efforts. Suicide is the leading cause of death among members of the U.S. military (Cox et al., 2011). For example, the Army and Marine Corp have suicide rates that are growing and already exceed those of the general population (Kuehn, 2010). To address this problem, all military branches have instituted suicide prevention policies and interventions, many of them focused on screening. The Army's Suicide Prevention Program is comprehensive as it identifies primary, secondary, and tertiary levels of prevention. Most of the training occurs at the primary level of prevention. The Applied Suicide Prevention Intervention Skills Training (ASIST) program is mandatory for all leaders, chaplains, and health and mental health professionals. It teaches these "gatekeepers," to identify signs of suicide and use appropriate interventions. The updated Health Promotion, Risk

Reduction, and Suicide Prevention (AR 600-63) regulation mandates that an appropriate number of gatekeeper trainers must be maintained.

The ASIST program was intended to complement the "Ask, Care, Escort" (ACE) suicide prevention training program, which is provided to all soldiers on an annual basis. The ACE program uses a buddy system, with soldiers taking care of soldiers. It teaches individuals how to identify risk factors for suicide as well as to provide information about the available resources. This training includes print resources such as the ACE tip cards.

The Department of Defense asked the Research and Development (RAND) Corporation to evaluate the existing military suicide prevention programs. RAND identified six characteristics found in effective suicide prevention programs. While military programs had some of these characteristics, no branch's program had all of them (RAND Corporation, 2010). One of the largest barriers to suicide prevention is the stigma associated with seeking help. In response, the military launched the Real Warriors Campaign, which provides service members with access to videos of other military employees sharing their positive experiences of seeking help (Department of Defense, 2011).

Suicide prevention for veterans has also been the subject of public policy. In 2004, the Office of Veterans Affairs (VA) drafted the Mental Health Strategic Plan (MHSP). This plan targeted the invisible wounds of war, including suicide risk. It presented more than 200 benchmarks, 10 of which were specific to suicide prevention (Department of VA, Office of Inspector General, 2007). The MHSP dictated that VA facilities meet compliance with all of these benchmarks in a 5-year period. Unfortunately, compliance with all of these benchmarks was not met within the allocated time frame.

Some of the VA benchmarks are similar to Army initiatives. For example, the VA requires suicide prevention training for all staff members who interact with veterans from physicians to telephone operators. In each VA facility, there is a suicide prevention coordinator responsible for coordinating training. Coordinators' additional responsibilities include identifying individuals at high risk for suicide and ensuring they have appropriate care.

The Joshua Omvig Veterans Suicide Prevention Act, passed in 2007, strengthened these efforts in the VA. This act provided for increased training for VA staff, an increased use of suicide assessments, designation of suicide prevention counselors, research on veteran's mental health, outreach for veterans and their families, and availability of 24-hour mental health care. This last provision resulted in the formation of the Veteran's Suicide Prevention Hotline.

Native American Suicide Prevention Law. Native Americans have the highest suicide rates of any ethnic minority (Anderson & Smith, 2003) with markedly higher suicide rates for young people, two to three times the national average (Strickland, Walsh, & Cooper, 2006). On March 31, 2011, Governor Susan Martinez of New Mexico signed the Native American Suicide Prevention Law. This law created a statewide clearinghouse for

Native American youth targeted suicide prevention and culturally based prevention programs and initiatives. Unfortunately, when this act was signed, the appropriate funding was not allocated.

Golden Gate Bridge Suicide Prevention Net. Restricting access to lethal means is an important element of suicide prevention that has been shown to be effective in reducing suicides (Mann et al., 2005). The Golden Gate Bridge (GGB) in San Francisco, California, is the most popular place to commit suicide in the world (Blaustein & Fleming, 2009). In 1939, only 2 years after the bridge opened, the California Highway Patrol officially asked the Golden Gate District to do something about the suicides. In 2008, the board of directors for the Golden Gate Transportation District voted to install a suicide prevention net after several different alternatives had been tested. The net has yet to be constructed, as it is currently pending funding. Suicide deterrent structures can be seen at various locations across the country, including the Empire State Building and Seattle's Aurora Avenue Bridge.

Gun Control. Another effective way to restrict access to lethal means is through gun control legislation. In the history of the United States, there have been various laws related to gun control. In 1968, the Gun Control Act was passed after the assassination of President Kennedy, Robert Kennedy, and Martin Luther King Jr. This legislation banned mail order shotgun and rifles. In 1994, the Brady Handgun Act was passed, requiring firearms dealers to perform a background check on individuals purchasing guns. The Gun Bill, passed in 1999, extends the same provisions for guns purchased at trade shows. This background check required a 5-day waiting period. This waiting period inadvertently acts as a buffer against impulsive decision making, which is often associated with suicide (Klonsky & May, 2010).

Prevention initiatives are moving closer to the forefront of the American public's attention. Due to the nature of mental disorders risk and protective factors, public laws, and policies dealing with prevention are quite diverse.

Questions for Discussion_____

1. Given what you know about the risk and protective factors for mental disorders, what are the policies that influence these disorders? How could they be improved? Should new policies be developed? What would they look like?

2. Identify some prevention programs for various disorders. How do you think that these programs could be implemented using public policies? Would a local, state, or federal policy be most feasible?

3. How do you think the political environment influences these policies?

4

The Formation of Public Policy

Case Studies

T his chapter presents four different case studies. Each demonstrates a unique phenomenon found in the policy-making process. The first case study, "The Process of Establishing Suicide Deterrents on the Golden Gate Bridge [GGB]," shows how, despite evidence, policies continue to go unimplemented. The second case study, "Mothers Against Drunk Driving's Impact on the Minimum Drinking Age Legislation," shows how a grassroots organization can gather force and change national legislation. The third case study, "DARE: An Examination of Research Versus Policy," demonstrates the impact that popularity can have on the continuation of a program. The final case study "Development of the Patient Protection and Affordable Care Act (PPACA)," demonstrates multiple attempts at implementing nationalized health care, how the current legislation was formed, and how it influences the coverage of mental health prevention services.

The GGB is the most popular site in the world to commit suicide (Blaustein & Fleming, 2009). Individuals have crossed over other equally fatal bridges to commit suicide there. In fact, individuals have traveled from all over the world to commit suicide at the site. Over the history of the bridge, more than 1,300 individuals have completed suicide by jumping off its tresses. This number is most likely an underestimation as many of the bodies have not been discovered, and it is likely that many individuals have jumped after sunset when the bridge is closed to pedestrian traffic.

Case Study 1: The Process of Establishing Suicide Deterrents on the GGB

This case study demonstrates how lengthy the establishment of legislative prevention interventions can be. Note the variety of different actors in the process.

The construction of GGB began on January 5, 1933. It was opened to the public on May 27, 1937. The bridge was initially designed with a 5.5-ft. tall fence. During construction, it was lowered to 4 ft. The reasons for this change are unknown. It is theorized that the chief engineer, Joseph Strauss, lowered the fences so that he could see over the railing as he stood only 5 ft. tall.

The suicides began not long after the bridge was opened to the public. Harrold Wobbler, a 47-year-old World War I veteran, was the first individual to commit suicide from the GGB, only 3 months after it was opened. Two years after the bridge was opened to the public, the California Highway Patrol officially asked the GGB Highway and Transportation District (District) to address the suicide problem. Individuals and groups have advocated for prevention measures over the past eight decades. Presented in this case study is a brief discussion of the history of attempts to implement suicide prevention measures, culminating with those for the current proposed suicide prevention net. This case study demonstrates the large amount of time and number of attempts required to establish policy change.

In 1940, the District's Board of Directors (Board) discussed the possible use of a suicide prevention screen. However, this alternative was abandoned due to aesthetic and financial concerns. These two concerns, along with the notion that individuals will find a means of committing suicide with a physical deterrent present, are repeatedly used over the history of advocacy attempts as the rationale for not implementing various suicide prevention alternatives.

The second official attempt to address suicides occurred in 1948. The Board commissioned a study of the suicide problem on the bridge. They examined the possibility of erecting a high fence. This proposal, submitted to the district's building and operations committee, was not acted on.

In 1954, a third attempt was made to deter suicides. Two suicide prevention barrier plans were proposed to the District's Building and Operating Committee. One option was the addition of a 2-ft. extension to the existing 4-ft. fence. The other option was a fence made of barbed wire extending 3 ft. above the existing fence. A section of barbed wire fence was placed near the toll plazas but was later removed, having been deemed to be hazardous for bridge workers.

The first nonphysical suicide prevention measure was installed in 1960. Closed-circuit television cameras were put in place to monitor traffic. Additional cameras were added in the mid-1990s and again after September 11, 2001. These cameras provide surveillance of the sidewalks. They are monitored 24 hours a day. They have been an important resource in the identification of potential suicides enabling trained bridge staff to intervene.

In 1964, the Board's Security Committee recommended a suicide prevention barrier. The next year, the board created a subcommittee of three security members to review applications for architectural engineers to create the proposed structure. This proposal lay dormant for 6 years.

In 1970, the District examined 18 different suicide prevention alternatives in conjunction with the Anshen & Allen Architectural Firm. Alternatives included a 9-ft. fence, a nylon safety net, and even high voltage laser beams. The District Board drafted a list of criteria for the evaluation of the proposed alternatives. They were as follows:

- Cannot cause safety or nuisance hazards to pedestrians or bridge personnel
- Must be totally effective as a barrier
- Cannot bar pedestrian traffic
- Weight cannot be beyond established allowable limits
- Cannot cause excessive maintenance problems
- Aerodynamics (wind stability) cannot be beyond established allowable limits.

Later the following criteria were added,

- Historical and architectural considerations
- Visual and aesthetic impacts
- Cost-effectiveness

The Board decided on a lightweight 8-ft. high rail with rods the size of a thick pencil as to avoid impeding the view. It was estimated to cost $800,000. A mock-up of the Anshen & Allen design was built and tested, but it was voted down because it proved to be scalable. The funds that were allocated for this project were redirected to reserves for ferries, terminals, replacement of cables, and future bridge repairs. The potential cost of implementing a suicide prevention barrier rose between $2 and $3 million dollars, and the Board attempted to seek outside funding. Shortly afterward, the matter was tabled.

In the meantime, media coverage intensified as the suicide numbers increased. Several newspapers had an ongoing count of the number of jumpers. In 1973, as the number approached 500, coverage reached a peak. Individuals raced to be the 500th. The actual 500th jumper was a commune dweller who was tripping on lysergic acid diethylamide, also known as LSD.

In 1977, the GGB directors addressed the issue again by proposing the installation of suicide deterrent railning when the existing railing was scheduled to be removed for sandblasting and repainting. However, the plan went nowhere.

On Memorial Day, 1977, only days after the 600th suicide, Reverend Jim Jones, who founded the Peoples Temple, organized an antisuicide rally. More than 400 antisuicide activists were present. Jones advocated for the installation of a barrier. In his speech, he spoke of the selfishness of committing suicide. Ironically, only 18 months later, he and 913 of his followers committed mass suicide in Guyana.

The matter of suicide prevention on the GGB lay dormant for several years. In 1994, the District adapted the existing emergency call boxes to accommodate suicide prevention measures. New phones were also added, bringing the total number of phones to 15. When used, callers are connected first to the Sergeant's office, where they can be immediately redirected to suicide prevention counselors and direct bridge staff to the area to intervene, depending on the type of caller.

By this time, the bridge had become the best known suicide site in the world. It almost appeared as if San Franciscans took pride in this notoriety. Tour busses announced the suicide numbers as they passed the bridge. The local papers kept a running tally of the number of jumpers and announced each leap. This phenomenon even reached a national coverage with several articles in *Newsweek* and *Time* magazines.

Media reports on this type of behavior have been shown to increase imitative behaviors (Beautrais, 2007). In 1995, as the number of suicides reached 1,000, the District did something: They stopped releasing the official count. The District feared that there would be a race to be the 1,000th jumper, similar to what happened in 1973, with the 500th jumper. The media was asked to stop coverage. Nevertheless, the *San Francisco Examiner* maintained its own count and publicized the 1,000th suicide.

The next year, the District Board attempted to address the issue again: They decided to repurpose the existing patrols on the bridge with one of their primary directives being suicide prevention. The Bridge Patrol surveys the bridge on foot and scooter. In 1999, bicycle patrols were added. These forces were increased after September 11, 2001. All of the security personnel, and several ironworkers, receive special training in suicide prevention. It is reported that patrols prevent 55 suicides a year.

In 1998, another physical deterrent was tested. In 1993, the Board approved testing for a flexible high tension wire fence by Z-Clip International Fencing Systems. It was designed to extend 6 ft. above the existing railing. When the initial design was tested, it was found that 5 of 14 individuals were able to climb over the barrier. Adjustments were made so that only one person made it over. An architectural advisory panel recommended against the device for aesthetic reasons. The fence was never installed because it did not meet the District's criteria of being "totally effective" as a deterrent.

In September of 2000, Kevin Hines took a death-defying jump from the GGB. The leap is almost inevitably fatal. However, the then 18-year-old Hines survived the leap. To date, only 34 individuals have survived. He reported that if there had been a suicide deterrent system that day in 2000, he would most likely have been caught trying to climb the fence. After this event, Kevin and his family became influential advocates for a physical suicide deterrent system.

Kevin was featured in Eric Steel's film *The Bridge*, which was filmed in 2004. This film depicted the suicide problem on the GGB. The filmmakers captured 19 suicides and many more attempts. They followed up with families and friends of the jumpers to get a broader perspective of the situation. Individuals spoke of mental illness and drug addiction frequently. During the filming, they played an instrumental role in preventing suicides, as they would contact the Bridge Authority when attempters were spotted. It also played a broader role in suicide prevention efforts on the bridge by notifying the larger public of the problem.

That same year, the District began to take action. They held a suicide prevention training run by San Francisco Suicide Prevention Inc. All security staff members were required, and ironworkers were welcomed to attend. A total of more than 120 staff members were present for this training.

The next year, the District instituted a policy resolving to implement a suicide prevention barrier on the GGB. This policy laid out the criteria for evaluating potential physical suicide deterrent systems. Previous policy guidelines for the evaluation of suicide prevention alternatives included criteria such as "must be *totally* effective as a barrier." The Board agreed that this criterion could be used to eliminate any suicide deterrent system. The newly adopted criteria are as follows:

- Must impede the ability of an individual to jump off the GGB
- Must not cause safety or nuisance hazards to sidewalk users, including pedestrians, bicyclists, District staff, and distract contractors/security partners
- Must be able to be maintained as a routine part of the District's ongoing Bridge maintenance program and without undue risk of injury to District employees
- Must not diminish ability to provide adequate security of the GGB
- Must continue to allow access to the underside of the Bridge for emergency response and maintenance activities
- Must not have a negative impact on the wind stability of the GGB
- Must satisfy requirement of state and federal historic preservation laws
- Must have minimal visual and aesthetic impacts on the GGB
- Must be cost-effective to construct and maintain
- Must not in and of itself create undue risk of injury to anyone who comes in contact with the suicide deterrent system
- Must not prevent construction of a moveable median barrier in the GGB (Board of Directors, 2005, April 22)

In addition to these guidelines, the Board instituted a policy regarding the funding of the project. They determined that they did not want it to be funded with the use of tolls.

In March of 2006, the planning process for the project began. The Board met to identify their plan of action for the GGB Suicide Deterrent Preliminary Engineering and Environmental Design Study. They initially decided to split the study into two different projects requiring two separate contracts. However, only 2 weeks after deciding to split the study into two separate projects, the board changed their minds. They decided that it was in their best interest to split the study into two separate phases. This would require the Board to have only one contract rather than two. It also allowed for a greater communication between the two projects. Phase 1 would include conducting a wind study of generic suicide deterrent concepts. Generic design concepts were said to fall into one of the three categories: (1) a net under the bridge, (2) a fence added to the existing railing, and (3) replacing the existing railing with a new structure. Phase 2 would be a full preliminary engineering, environmental, and historical preservation study, which would include determining a cost estimate for the construction of the proposed alternatives.

During these meetings, the Board discussed the funding requirements. The study was projected to cost $2 million. The Metropolitan Transportation Commission (MTC) committed to funding $1.6 million of the project. This funding had stipulations requiring the District to produce 20% of the money, or $400,000, before the funding would be released. The funding came from several sources. An amount of $25,000 was provided by the County of Marin, $100,000 came from the City and County of San Francisco, $18,700 came from numerous donors through the Psychiatric Foundation of Northern California, and $10,000 came from other private sources producing only $153,700 of the required $400,000 to fund the project. In April of 2006, the MTC amended their initial agreement and provided the additional $250,000 required to fund the project.

The next step was for the District to identify a contractor to carry out the two phases of the project. They opened the request for proposals on June 28, 2006. All proposals were due on August 1 of that same year. On September 22, the District's Board announced that the contract had been awarded to DMJM Harris.

The first phase of the study started shortly after the contract was awarded. DMJM Harris tested more than 60 different variations of the three different forms of suicide deterrents. The testing determined that any addition to the bridge would compromise its wind stability. However, additional measures could be added to the bridge to mitigate this problem. They were able to identify six different viable alternatives that met the board's criteria: (1) add an additional 8-ft. vertical barrier to the existing railing, (2) add an 8-ft. vertical barrier to the existing railing, (3) replace the existing railing with a 12-ft. vertical barrier, (4) replace the existing railing with a 12-ft. horizontal barrier, (5) add a net system that extends horizontally from the bridge, and (6) build nothing.

The next phase of the study began in June of 2007. This endeavor was much more complex than the first phase of the project. It was slated to take 18 months. This portion of the study examined a multitude of aspects, including the preliminary engineering and environmental analysis, the visual analysis, the historical preservation evaluation, and the preparation of cost estimates. Once the results were obtained, they were released to the public for review.

After the document was released to the public, there was a 7-week period where the public was able to voice their opinions to the Board, which would be taken into consideration in their final decision. The Board received comments both in paper and electronic form. In addition, two public hearings were held in San Francisco and San Rafael. The public was only marginally in favor of some form of physical deterrent with 50.13% voicing opinions in favor.

Shortly after the 7-week period elapsed, Mayor Newsom and an advisory board composed of architects and engineers suggested that the District pursue alternative means to a suicide barrier. This was a position that contrasted with the city's previous stance on the matter. They argued that the money could be better spent on training employees and volunteers to be more equipped in suicide prevention techniques. However, this advisory board conceded that if a suicide deterrent system were to be implemented, the netting system would be the most suitable as it does not detract from the aesthetics or integrity of the structure. The California Highway Patrol was opposed to the netting, as construction would lead to lengthy traffic delays and require extensive officer training.

Amid significant public controversy, the Board identified the netting system as the preferred alternative on October 10, 2008. This decision provided the board with some direction required for three tasks: (1) responding to community member comments, (2) preparing a Memorandum of Agreement, and (3) conducting additional studies such as an avian study. The second two portions would be incorporated into the final Environmental Impact Report and the Findings of No Significant Impacts Report.

The Memorandum of Agreement was a necessary step in the completion of this project, as the GGB has been identified as a historic site since 1980. Adding a net system to the bridge is identified as an "adverse effect." As a result, an agreement among the California Department of transportation, the California State Historic Preservation Officer, and the Federal Advisory Council on Historic Preservation was necessary to maintain federal funding for the project. On July 19, 2009, the Memorandum of Agreement was approved by all agencies. It resulted in some small changes to the project, including the anticipated color of the net.

After this Memorandum of Agreement was signed, the plans for the suicide prevention net were finalized. This allowed the Board to draft the final Environmental Impact Report and Environmental Analysis, incorporating all of the changes that were made as a result of the Memorandum of Agreement. This report outlined the impact of the project on four key resources: (1) visual/aesthetic, (2) historic, (3) biological, and (4) cultural. They determined that the biological impacts could be mitigated. However, the other areas would inevitably be affected by the implementation of the net. The board agreed that the benefits outweighed the consequences. The Board released the final report in January 2010 and certified it the next month.

The actual construction of the netting system is tied to funding. The net alternative is projected to cost $50 million. In 2005, the Board instituted a policy stating that tolls would not be used to gather the funding necessary for the construction of the net system. Funding has proven to be a considerable issue. In August of 2010, the MTC presented $5 million to the District Board. It will be used for the design phase of the netting system. As yet, the sources of the additional $45 million have not been identified.

This is as far as a suicide prevention measure has gone on the GGB. However, the bridge's lengthy history of failed attempts is a remaining cause of concern. With considerable amounts of national attention, hopefully, this project will be seen to fruition, which may save the lives of thousands of people.

Historic sites around the world such as the Sydney Harbor Bridge, the Empire State Building, and the Eiffel Tower have been deemed suicide magnets. All of these places have implemented suicide prevention measures that have eliminated or reduced suicides to a mere handful. Skeptics may claim that if individuals are sincere in their attempts at suicide, they will commit it by using another means. One study (Miller, Azarel, & Hemenway, 2006) showed that 34% of individuals believed that if a suicide prevention barrier was placed on the GGB, *every single jumper* would find another means of committing suicide; 40% believed that most would find another means. However, a study conducted by Seiden (1978) shows that this is untrue. This study followed 515 people who had attempted suicide on the bridge between 1937 and 1971. At the time of the study, 94% of the would-be suicides were either still alive or had died of natural causes, which demonstrates the acute nature of suicide.

For an up-to-date discussion of the progress of the GGB Physical Suicide Deterrent System Project, visit the project's website at http://www.ggbsuicide barrier.org/.

Discussion Questions

1. How do you feel about implementing the net system under the GGB? Do you think that it will be effective? How do you think that the feelings of public stakeholders affected the process of implementing the policy?

2. What could stakeholders have done to get the net policy in place sooner?

3. Do you think that the net will actually be built? Why or why not?

Case Study 2: Mothers Against Drunk Driving's Impact on Legislation

This case study demonstrates the impact that an organization can have on the policy development and implementation process.

Mothers Against Drunk Driving (MADD) has been one of the most influential nonprofit organizations, and they attribute their success to their approach. Initially, the cause was recognized because they shared their personal experiences of losing innocent children and loved ones instead of sharing statistics. This case study presents the development of the organization and their impact on the National Minimum Drinking Age Act.

MADD was founded in 1980 by Candy Lightner after her daughter, Cari, was killed by a repeat offender drunk driver. Candy learned of the circumstances of her daughter's death on the day of her daughter's funeral while passing by the site of the accident. It was the driver's fifth offense in 4 years. While talking to the officers who were investigating the case, she learned that it was unlikely that he would go to jail, let alone prison, for Cari's death. Candy went to judges and state agencies and got the run around. Candy became infuriated and decided to do something to address the issue. She formed Mothers Against Drunk Drivers (later Drivers was replaced with Driving and the acronym, MADD, came into use).

MADD began in Cari's still decorated bedroom with Candy and her friend Sue. They gathered information, found other victims, answered questions, sent newsletters, and contacted politicians. It was not long before the two of them had more than they could handle. Speaking engagements and media requests flooded in.

On September 5, 1980, MADD was incorporated on what would have been Cari's 14th birthday. This enabled them to start taking donations, which began trickling in at $5 and $10 increments from families. Across the country, another mother, Cindy Lamb, was heralding her own campaign against drunk driving. The previous year she had been hit by a drunk driver with her 5.5-month-old daughter, Laura, in the car. It was the driver's fifth offense in 4 years. The crash caused Laura to become the youngest paraplegic as a result of a drunk driving accident. After Cindy discovered the alcohol involvement in the accident, she began a letter writing campaign to law enforcement, judges, and senators. In 1980, she opened the Maryland chapter of MADD, and the public took note.

Candy and Cindy met on Capitol Hill for MADD's first national press conference on October 1, 1980. Their voices were heard across the country. Stories about MADD sprung up on news reports, in newspapers, and in magazines. The organization touched the hearts of Americans, including those that were in positions of authority, to do something to resolve the issue.

Not long after MADD was formed, it faced its first big legislative battle: changing the national minimum drinking age to 21. It was an uphill fight that would take 4 years. During this time period, MADD would have an impact on three areas that contributed to the passing of the legislation: (1) increased public awareness of the dangers of underage drinking, (2) changes in public attitudes toward underage drinking, and (3) lobbying for change.

The stage for change had already been set. From 1969 until 1976, 30 states lowered the minimum age to purchase alcohol because the voting age was lowered from 21 to 18 years with the 26th Amendment. Research began mounting, suggesting a dangerous relationship between drinking at age 18 and fatal traffic accidents. As a result, during the period from 1976 to 1980, 13 states raised their drinking ages, generally by 1 year.

MADD began lobbying at the state and local levels to push for more change. They buttonholed congressmen and flooded their offices with letters and telegrams. In 1981, more than 40 laws regarding drunk driving were passed. Eventually the matter came to national attention.

On April 14, 1982, President Reagan established the Presidential Commission Against Drunk Driving (Executive Order 12358) in response to the public outcry created by MADD. It comprises 26 members appointed by President Reagan and 2 representatives from both the House and the Senate. Candy Lightner was appointed as a member of the Commission. The Commission had 4 functions: (1) to increase public awareness of the seriousness of drunk driving; (2) to encourage communities to attack the drunk driving problem in a systematic manner, including adapting the legal process of prosecuting individuals with drunk driving charges; (3) to encourage states to adopt the latest techniques to resolve the problem; and (4) to generate public support for increased enforcement of drunk driving laws.

This Commission established 39 recommendations, one of which was the raising of the minimum legal purchasing age to 21 years. It was originally intended to target adult drunk driving, but it soon heralded the campaign to reduce underage drinking. The other 38 recommendations, including youth education and public information campaigns, soon fell into the background of public awareness.

The Commission initially proposed rewarding states for complying with the recommendations to increase the minimum drinking age to 21 years. However, a year after the recommendations were posed, only 4 of the 23 states had complied with the recommendation to implement a minimum drinking age of 21 years. It became clear that the legislation was necessary to get states to comply with the recommendation.

Candy Lightner gained the support of Representative Jim Howard (R-NJ) who introduced HR 5504. This legislation proposed an amendment to the Transportation Bill that would provide funding for highway and transportation projects. On June 7, 1984, the House voted 297 to 73 in favor of adopting the bill.

A similar bill was drafted in the Senate (S 2527). However, it became caught up in controversy. As a result, Senator Frank Lautenberg (D-NJ), chose to add it to HR 4616, a bill amending the Highway and Transportation Act of 1982, instead of HR 5504. This amendment proposed that states be punished for not complying with the minimum drinking age of 21 years.

A debate ensued between Lautenberg's proposal to punish states and Senator Gordon Humphrey (R-NH), who proposed that states be rewarded for complying with the legislation. The Senate voted, and there was overwhelming support for Lautenberg's proposal. After the Senate's approval of

Lautenberg's amendment, the bill was silently passed in the House. This made the minimum drinking age public law on June 28, 1984.

On July 17, 1984, President Reagan, signed the National Minimum Drinking Age Act into law. Reagan initially opposed the bill. However, he was up for reelection and made no secret that he believed that signing the legislation would improve his standing with voters.

The legislation required that all states comply with the new law by October 1, 1986, or risk losing 5% of their funding for highways. At the time of its signing, 23 states had minimum drinking ages below 21 years. Additionally, 9 states had laws that allowed individuals under the age of 21 to purchase beer and wine. By October 1, 1986, all states, except Idaho, Louisiana, Ohio, and Wyoming, had complied with the legislation. Those states that did not comply with the legislation by October 1, 1987, risked losing 10% of their funding. By 1988, all of the states had complied. This same legislation applied to U.S. territories. However, there was not strong support for this legislation in these areas. Guam adopted a minimum drinking age of 21 in 2010. To date, Puerto Rico and the Virgin Islands have drinking ages of 18, and as a result, they lose 10% of their highway funding annually.

The passing of this legislation has proven to be effective. Alcohol-related driving fatalities dropped from 48% in 1982 to 32% in 2009 (U.S. Department of Transportation [USDOT], National Highway Traffic Safety Administration [NHTSA], 2010). It is estimated that 27,677 lives have been saved between 1975 and 2009 as a result of the minimum drinking age legislation (USDOT, NHTSA, 2010).

After the passing of the National Minimum Drinking Age Act, MADD went on to play a part in the passing of several laws related to drunk driving. They had a hand in the passing of legislation, making it illegal to drive with a blood alcohol content above .08, dram shop laws that make establishments liable for the individuals to whom they sell alcohol, and many, many more. During the organizations' first 5 years of existence (1980–1985), 500 new laws addressing drunk driving were passed.

MADD attributes their success to several factors. One of these factors is their passionate, dedicated volunteers (MADD, 2005). During this 5-year period, the MADD organization exploded to become one of the largest grassroots organizations targeting alcohol in the nation. They began with only one chapter in California in 1980, expanding to 330 chapters in 47 states in 1985 (Marshall & Oleson, 1994).

Another tool that the organization used to gain success was the media (MADD, 2005). The media carried the MADD's very personal message, that the individuals killed in drunk driving accidents were somebody's child, partner, and friend, into the homes of millions of Americans. This message helped educate the public on the dangers of drunk driving. In addition, the media repeatedly came to MADD as a source of information, strengthening the organization's image as an expert resource.

In addition, the organization claims that their dedication to their mission has had a significant impact on their success (MADD, 2005). MADD continues to work toward their mission of supporting victims, stopping drunk driving, and preventing underage drinking. They have two strategies for reducing underage drinking: (1) Work with police departments to strengthen enforcement of minimum drinking age laws and (2) support and supply resources for a national media campaign on underage drinking.

Discussion Questions

1. In what ways do you think that this legislation could have been improved?

2. What can you take from this case study and apply to another issue?

3. Do you think that the factors that MADD attributes to their success (e.g., passionate volunteers, working with the media, and mission focus) are necessary for success?

Case Study 3: DARE: An Examination of Research Versus Policy

Drug Abuse Resistance Education (DARE) is the most widely used substance use prevention program in the United States. DARE's mission is to "provide children with the information and skills they need to live drug and violence free lives" (DARE, 2011). This mission statement is carried out through collaboration between police forces and school districts, with police officers teaching various curricula designed for elementary, middle, and high school classrooms. Typically, the program is introduced to students in fifth or sixth grade.

Since the program's founding in 1983, it has spread across the country and the world. The curriculum is reportedly taught in 72% of American school districts and 44 countries (DARE, 2009). The program is estimated to cost three quarters of a billion dollars in tax payer money annually (McNeal & Hanson, 1995). There's only one problem: Over the program's history, it has repeatedly been shown to be ineffective at accomplishing its primary objective, to reduce substance use behaviors of participants (West & O'Neal, 2004). Discussed in this case study is the history of the program, its development and adaptations, and its lack of support. Despite all of these factors, the program continues to be implemented.

During the early 1980s, it was clear to some that the war on drugs' target on the supply side of the drug trade was doing little to curb the American drug problem. Several projects were in place around the country to try to develop drug prevention programs. Project Self-Management and Resistance

Training (SMART) was one of these programs. It was being studied at the University of Southern California and tested in the Los Angeles Unified School District (LAUSD). Researchers were testing two different curricula: One was an "affective" program, focusing on building self-esteem and goal-setting, the other was a "resistance training" program, where students were taught about social pressures.

In 1983, the Los Angeles Police Department's Police Chief, Daryl Gates, approached LAUSD and asked it to be a part of the project. The researchers at Project SMART refused to amend their curricula to include uniformed police officers, so Dr. Ruth Rich, LAUSD's health education specialist, decided to join forces with Daryl Gates and develop their own program. They combined the two different SMART curricula, and DARE was born.

The pilot program began in September 1983 with 10 officers teaching in LAUSD fifth and sixth grade classes. Each of these officers taught students about the dangers of drugs, how to identify them, and strategies for resistance. The results of the pilot study were promising (Nyre, 1985). Interestingly, the study never reported on the substance use behaviors of participants.

Demand for drug prevention programs was high. The Nancy Reagan "Just Say No" campaign, warning children of the dangers of drug abuse, was in full swing. By 1985, the DARE program was used throughout LAUSD. There were several other drug prevention programs in existence competing for placement in schools. There was only one thing standing in the way of the DARE program's expansion; it had never been reviewed by independent researchers.

Dr. William DeJong was sent in by the National Institute of Justice (NIJ) to review the project. His study showed that "students who had DARE training reported significantly lower use of alcohol, cigarettes, and other drugs" 1 year after they received the program (DeJong, 1987, p. 279). These results, in addition to the fact that DARE was based in Project SMART, led the NIJ to provide the stamp of approval for the DARE program. As a result, the Bureau of Justice Assistance awarded the DARE program a $140,000 grant. A grant of this size is useful to support a local program. However, it's not enough to implement a program nationally.

In 1986, a solution presented itself. Congress passed the Drug Free Schools and Communities Act. As a part of this legislation, grant money was provided for the implementation of drug abuse prevention programs. Of the money allocated for programs, 10% was to be used for programs taught by uniformed police officers in the classroom, an area in which DARE had cornered the market. As the funding expanded, so did the curricula offered by DARE. They launched middle school and high school curricula in 1986 and 1988, respectively.

DARE went national. To support the growing organization, DARE America was formed in 1987. Officer training centers began popping up across the country.

Over the next 5 years, several studies were published on the effectiveness of the DARE program. These studies showed that DARE had no significant effect in reducing substance use behaviors of participants (e.g., Ringwalt, Ennett, & Holt, 1990). The only instance of a study supporting the program was the study published by Dr. DeJong, and it was criticized as being empirically flawed (Clayton, Catarello, & Walden, 1991). However, DARE America claimed that the program worked, using studies of the program's popularity as support (Bureau of Justice Assistance, 1991). In 1991, the Departments of Education and Justice commissioned a study from the Research Triangle Institute (RTI) to clarify the matter.

In 1993, a preliminary report of the RTI report was released at a conference in San Diego. The study (Ennett, Tobler, Ringwalt, & Flewelling, 1994) showed that the DARE program had little impact on substance use behaviors. The researchers found that interactive substance use prevention programs showed greater reductions in substance use behaviors when compared with DARE. But this wasn't to say that the program was completely ineffective. It was shown to teach children resistance skills and improve relationships between children and police officers.

The Ennet et al. (1994) study was published amid great controversy. The DARE organization publicly attacked researchers. Glenn Levant, President of DARE, claimed that "[researchers] don't want our police officers to do the work because they want it for themselves" (Miller, 2001). Publication on the matter could be found in national publications like *USA Today* and *The New York Times*. DARE began losing support.

In 1994, the Drug Free Schools and Communities Act was amended. The new legislation, the Safe and Drug Free Schools and Communities Act, required programs that received funds through this legislation be designed to reduce substance use among students as well as reduce violence. DARE was cited in the legislation as one of the "authorized activities" (Section 4116).

In this same year, DARE began implementing a new elementary curriculum called "DARE to Resist Drugs and Violence." Lessons on violence prevention, tobacco use, and terrorism were added to the DARE curriculum. In addition, the program abandoned the traditional lecture-based instruction and began emphasizing group exercises such as group discussion and role playing. Over the years, DARE America had been resistant to say that there were any problems with their program, the effectiveness of which was not supported by most prior research. After the program changed, DARE officials claimed that prior research was on an outdated program and therefore invalid.

The change in DARE programming seemed to come too late. DARE programs began to be dropped across the country. Seattle Police Chief, Norm Stamper, was particularly vocal, calling the program an "enormous failure." The media attention on the program swelled.

Research regarding DARE's effectiveness continued to mount. In February of 1997, RTI published the longitudinal study of the DARE program (Silvia,

Thorne, & Tashjian, 1997). This study demonstrated that DARE showed no reductions in substance use behaviors. In addition, they found that there was a great level of inconsistency with program implementation, even within school districts.

Rosenbaum and Hanson (1998) found similar results to those discovered by RTI. DARE increased participant's knowledge about drugs, improved their attitudes toward the police, and increased their ability to resist peer pressure to use illegal drugs. However, these changes wore off within 1 to 2 years. What was more upsetting is that the study found that the DARE program increased substance use among suburban youth by 3% to 5%.

In March of 1997, the U.S. Government Accountability Office (1997) examined the efforts to reduce the American drug problem. One of the elements that they examined was research on promising school-based drug prevention programs. Individual programs that showed promise were listed; DARE was not among them.

Amid mounting research and public concern that the DARE program didn't work, Congress started to take action to push the DARE program to revamp their curriculum. The Department of Education proposed new Principles of Effectiveness for the programs that received funding under the Safe and Drug Free Schools and Communities Act. This amendment to the legislation had several requirements for grantees:

- Programs must be based on a thorough assessment of objective data about the drug and violence problems in the schools and communities served.
- Programs must design their activities to meet their measureable goals and objectives for drug and violence prevention.
- Programs must design and implement their activities based on research or evaluation that provides evidence that the strategies used prevent or reduce drug use, violence, or disruptive behavior among youth.
- Programs must be evaluated periodically to assess their progress toward achieving their goals and objectives, and use their evaluation results to refine, improve, and strengthen their program and to refine their goals and objectives as appropriate.

Programs had 2 years to meet these requirements, or they would not receive future funding. It was clear that the DARE program would have to make changes in order to maintain its funding. Many school districts began to drop or scale back their DARE programs.

Additional pressure was received from the Department of Justice. The 1998 budget included some interesting language, crafted by the House Subcommittee on Commerce, Justice, State, and the Judiciary. It stated, "Recent studies indicate the need for the program to adapt to the changing culture within our schools. The committee directs the Department to work with officials with the DARE America Program to create new and more effective course criteria" (Senate Report 105-48, 105th Congress, 1997).

The controversy between researchers and DARE administrators reached a boiling point. The U.S. Departments of Justice and Education called a meeting between researchers and DARE administrators in May 1998. Several federal government officials were present, including Bill Modzeleik, the head of the Department of Education's Safe and Drug-Free Schools Program. By the end of the meeting, it seemed that DARE was willing to make peace with the research community.

After the meeting, the Robert Wood Johnson Foundation approached the DARE program about their curriculum. They saw potential in the DARE network, which they saw as having an impressive infrastructure, unlike any other in the country. DARE was in 70% of the schools throughout the country. In addition, they were training hundreds of officers every year. Because of these factors, the Robert Wood Johnson Foundation thought it made sense to revise the program rather than replace it (Berman & Fox, 2009).

In 1999, the Robert Wood Johnson Foundation agreed to commit $13.7 million over a 5-year period. Rather than provide the funds directly to the DARE program, they had the funds administered by Zili Sloboda at the University of Akron. Working with Dr. Sloboda, DARE agreed to make some changes to the curriculum. This new program, called "Take Charge of Your Life," consisted of ten 45-minute lessons delivered in seventh grade and seven booster lessons delivered in ninth grade. This program was less instruction based and more interactive than previous programs.

In 2000, every DARE officer in the country was retrained to work with the new curriculum. Dr. Sloboda undertook an ambitious study to examine the impact of the "Take Charge of Your Life" program on more than 14,000 students in Detroit, Houston, Los Angeles, New Orleans, Newark, and St. Louis.

> DARE seized the opportunity for some positive press. Glenn Levant told *The New York Times*, "There's quite a bit that we can do to make [the curriculum] better and we realize it." He went on to add, "I'm not saying it was effective, but it was state of the art when we launched it. Now it's time for science to improve upon what we're doing." (Zernike, 2001, p. 1)

DARE began to see some mixed attention with regard to funding. In 2000, the Department of Justice's Bureau of Justice Assistance provided $2 million to DARE. In addition, the Department of Education gave $439 million to each state, which was to be allocated for substance abuse prevention programs under the Safe and Drug Free Schools and Communities Act. However, the Department of Education said that it would no longer allow schools to spend money on programs like DARE, which lacked empirical support.

The initial results for the study on the "Take Charge of Your Life" curriculum were released in 2002. They were encouraging, showing that students who participated in the program showed improved drug refusal skills and more negative attitudes toward drug than participants in the control groups. "It shows us that the program is doing what it was intended to do, and in a very significant way," Sloboda told a reporter from Associated Press (2005).

The researchers hoped that the effect would hold up in the long term. However, there were some major complications that hindered the study. Hurricane Katrina devastated New Orleans, and many of the study participants ended up in Houston. In addition, they found that there was contamination in the control group, as many control group participants had received some form of drug prevention education.

In 2002, the Department of Education published its list of exemplary or promising drug and violence prevention programs at the request of Congress in 1994 (Department of Education, 2002). "Exemplary programs" were those that were shown to be effective through empirical data. "Promising programs" were those that had sufficient evidence demonstrating the potential for positive outcomes. In 2001, when the panel released their results, they had identified 9 exemplary programs and 33 promising programs. DARE was not included in either list.

In January of 2003, the U.S. Government Accountability Office (2003) released another report on drug prevention programs. This time they mentioned DARE by name. The writers of the report examined six different longitudinal studies of DARE. All of the studies showed that it had no long-term impact in reducing substance use. In fact, there were instances where substance use behavior increased in participants.

In 2006, the Surgeon General released a "Call to Action to Prevent and Reduce Underage Drinking" (Office of the Surgeon General, 2006). This report discussed the federal effort to address the issue, which was coordinated by the Interagency Coordinating Committee on the Prevention of Underage Drinking. The report highlighted programs that were supported by the coordinating committee and various government branches. DARE was listed as a program supported by the Department of Defense.

Research reporting on the effectiveness of the "Take Charge of Your Life" curriculum started coming in. It was shown to significantly increase alcohol and tobacco use by participants (Sloboda et al., 2009). The organization recognized that they needed to change their curriculum. In 2007, DARE reached an agreement with the Pennsylvania State University to use their "Keepin it REAL" curriculum, which had met the Substance Abuse and Mental Health Services Administration's (SAMHSA) guidelines for an evidence-based program in 2006. This curriculum is taught over 10 weeks with 45-minute sessions taught once a week and booster sessions taught the following year. Students are taught the risks associated with substance abuse, strategies for resistance, and antidrug normative beliefs and attitudes. This is the first time that DARE had a government-approved and research-backed program. However, the programs targeting elementary school– and high school–aged children and the after-school programs continue to not meet SAMHSA's requirements.

DARE did not come out of the public debate on its effectiveness unscathed. Several school districts throughout the country dropped the program. In addition, the DARE program has, in large part, lost its ability to receive federal funding because it has demonstrated a lack of empirical support for its programs. Despite this, the DARE program continues to be taught throughout the country and across the world. This is made possible because DARE receives funding through private donations and sales of their products, and it has even been included within the budget of several police departments.

Research by Birkeland, Murphy-Graham, and Weiss (2005) demonstrated that school administrators had good reasons for continuing to implement the DARE program despite poor reviews from researchers. The main reason that administrators continued the program was because of improved relationships between police officers and students. Other rationales were also included in explanations such as improved relationships between schools and police forces.

This case study demonstrates the gap between the research and policy. Research does not always affect public policy. Repeatedly, DARE was shown to fail to meet its primary objective of reducing substance use behaviors of adolescents, yet it continues to be implemented. Some researchers have argued that evaluation research rarely has an impact on policy makers (Weiss, Murphy-Graham, Petrosino, & Gandhi, 2008). The factor limiting the impact of research on public policy is that it often takes years to complete a good evaluation of a program, a timeline not shared by most policy makers.

Discussion Questions

1. What have you learned about the policy process from this case study? Can you apply that to other potential policies?

2. Why do you think this program continues to be implemented in schools? How can these policies be changed? Is there a better alternative? What would that look like?

3. Do you think that universal programs (those targeting large populations such as school children) are as effective as smaller programs that are tailored to the group they target (e.g., school children in Indianapolis, Indiana)? Why or why not? How could this type of program be implemented through policy?

Case Study 4: Development of the PPACA _____

Health care reform has been an area of significant controversy over the years. Since the beginning of the 1900s, presidential administrations have been attempting to implement nationalized health care (The Henry J. Kaiser Family Foundation [THJKFF], 2009). However, they have never been completely successful. All that changed on March 23, 2010, when the Obama administration passed the PPACA (P.L. 111-148). This legislation has requirements that states provide subsidized health care coverage, businesses provide health care options, and individuals carry personal health insurance. Incorporated within the legislation are several aspects that touch on prevention in health care, including a national strategy for prevention and wellness (THJKFF, 2010a). This area of the legislation expands the requirements for coverage on preventative services. With this legislation, it is important to understand that mental health is an aspect of health. For example, grants were made available for mental health prevention services starting in 2010. In addition, the legislation mandates that coverage be provided for mental health services by 2014, including preventative services (SAMHSA, 2010). Discussed in this case study is the history of attempts at nationalized health insurance, the history and development of the PPACA, and the proposals for the future.

A Brief History of Nationalized Health Care Attempts

The presidential campaign of 1912 is the first time in the nation's history that a nationalized health care coverage became a matter of debate. Theodore Roosevelt, the running mate for the Progressive Party, also known as the Bull Moose Party, advocated for what is currently known as the welfare state. He supported the implementation of nationalized health coverage, modeled after the legislation passed in Great Britain (Feldman, 2000) and Germany (Ross, 2002). The Progressive Party had two rationales for the implementation of insurance. First, by providing sick pay, insurance would eliminate sickness as a cause of poverty. Second, insurance would reduce the costs of treatment, which would create incentives for disease prevention (Ross, 2002). After losing the election, the Progressive Party advocated for state based systems of mandatory health insurance in eight states (THJKFF, 2009). However, this legislation was largely abandoned at the start of World War I (Ross, 2002). The notion of insurance was stigmatized throughout the nation due to its roots in Germany.

In 1926, the Committee on the Costs of Medical Care was formed due to concerns about the cost and distribution of medical care (Ross, 2002). Eight philanthropic organizations, including the Rockefeller Foundation, joined together and created a team that was composed of 50 economists, physicians, public health specialists, and public interest groups (Palmer, 1999). The group proposed that more national resources be allocated for health care and viewed voluntary health insurance as a means of covering the costs. They were met with significant opposition, which included the American Medical Association.

The Great Depression brought renewed interest in nationalized health insurance. There was a growing lower class, with as much as 25% of

Americans being unemployed. Sickness was the leading cause of poverty (THJKFF, 1999). This was partially explained by the rise in medical costs, which was justified by the cost of educating physicians (Ross, 2002). Citizens groups began to form to advocate for change. President Roosevelt responded in 1934 by forming the Committee on Economic Security, which was to create a program to address unemployment and old-age issues, as well as health insurance and medical care. The initial draft of the Social Security Act included regulations on national health insurance. However, this element was left out of the final draft of the legislation as unemployment and old-age benefits took priority (Palmer, 1999). Despite this, the Social Security Act did have a positive impact on health care for the less advantaged, providing funds to states to expand public health care. Attempts were made a few years later to institute nationalized health care. However, the Democratic majority in the House and Senate became divided over expansion of the government, and the legislation was struck down in 1938 (THJKFF, 1999).

During World War II, production of wartime goods was of central importance. President Roosevelt created the National War Labor Board in January 1942 to resolve labor disputes. He placed a cap on wages. To circumvent the wage ceiling and attract workers, employers began to offer fringe benefits such as health insurance and pensions, which were not paid in cash and thus were not incorporated into the wage. Roosevelt had plans of establishing a nationalized health care coverage at the end of the war.

After the war ended, President Truman proposed nationalized health care coverage as a part of his "Fair Deal" agenda. Truman believed that everyone should have access to health care. In addition, he believed that the health of America's youth, similar to their education, was the responsibility of the American public (Harry S. Truman Library and Museum, 2011). He proposed doing this by addressing several areas in the Wagner-Murray-Dingell Bill. First, he aimed to increase the number of medical professionals in rural areas by providing them with federal incentives. Second, he cited the need for higher quality health coverage in lower economic areas. He believed that this would be possible by providing federal funds for the construction of new hospitals. Third, he proposed the creation of a board of doctors and government officials to establish a set of regulations and standards for hospitals and medical professionals. Last, he proposed a voluntary system of nationalized health insurance. The American Medical Association vehemently attacked the legislation deeming it a shift toward communism, which incited fear in the American public of governmental control. The legislation quickly began losing support. After the launch of the Korean War, Truman was forced to abandon the bill.

It wasn't until the 1960s that nationalized health insurance was addressed again in the public arena as a result of the failure of employer-based health insurance to provide affordable health care for the sick and elderly. In 1960, Congress passed the Kerr-Mills Act, which provided states with grants to cover health care of the elderly poor. While this legislation sounded good in principle, it failed in practice. By 1963, only 28 states were participating in the grant program, and many of them had not budgeted their funds effectively.

In 1964, President Johnson was elected with health coverage as one of his major platforms. By 1965, there were several proposals to ameliorate the issues presented by the Kerr-Mills Act. Wilbur Mills, a Southern Democrat and head of the House Ways and Means Committee, helped draft proposals for the Medicare and Medicaid legislation with elements of each of the proposals presented by the Kerr-Mills Act. Previously, this type of legislation had been blocked from passing by Southern Democrats due to issues of expansion of governmental control and its influence on segregation. However, Mills, who was previously against the legislation, tempered the attitudes of Southern congressmen, and the legislation passed as a part of the Social Security Act. Since the passing of the legislation, Medicare and Medicaid have become one of the largest providers of coverage for mental illness services. However, the passage of this legislation had other unintended impacts on the mental health care. It increased difficulties in receiving long-term care, resulting in deinstitutionalization of a large number of individuals in this type of treatment (Stevens, Rosenburg, & Burns, 2006).

In the 1970s, rising health care costs began to become a concern. Senator Ted Kennedy campaigned across the country about the "Health Care Crisis in America" in an effort to gain support for his nationalized health insurance plan. Kennedy's plan, the "Health Security Act," proposed a universal single-payer plan with no co-pays to be financed through payroll taxes.

In 1971, President Nixon countered Kennedy's plan with a nationalized health coverage plan of his own. His plan, called the "Comprehensive Health Insurance Plan," was expanded in 1974. The proposal would replace Medicaid covering the working poor and unemployed. In addition, it provided a universal program with voluntary employer participation. The proposal was cosponsored by Representative Mills, who was still the head of the House Ways and Means Committee. Instead of fighting the legislation, Kennedy teamed up with Mills to produce a middle-ground proposal. There was a significant controversy within congress about the appropriate measures for the legislation. The proposals were soon overshadowed by the Watergate scandal. Despite President Ford's support of nationalized health coverage, his proposals failed to come to the House floor due to lack of consensus.

During his campaign, President Carter pledged to support nationalized health care coverage. However, once he reached office, he shifted his focus from nationalized health coverage to cost containment due to a weakened economy. Senator Kennedy became impatient for a new plan for nationalized health coverage and decided to draft a new proposal. Kennedy's new proposal called for competition between private insurance companies for customers who would receive a card to use for medical treatment from physicians and hospitals. The cost of the card was on a sliding scale depending on income, and employers were responsible for carrying a majority of the costs;

rates were to be set on actuarial risks. A month after Kennedy's plan was unveiled, President Carter released his proposal. He advocated that employers should provide minimum coverage, expansion of coverage for the poor and elderly, and a new public corporation that would provide services to everyone else. Congress was becoming increasingly conservative after the Watergate scandal. Neither proposal stood much of a chance. To fend off legislation mandating cost containment, hospitals began to voluntarily implement methods for managing their costs (THJKFF, 2009).

Nationalized health care would not become a national issue again until the 1990s. The surprise election of Pennsylvania Senator Harris Wofford, who was a large proponent of nationalized health care, signaled that the time was ripe for the issue to be presented again. A large number of proposals began surfacing in the early 1990s. During the 1992 presidential election, candidate Bill Clinton proposed the Health Security Act. The plan proposed universal coverage with employer and individual mandates. Coverage would be provided by private insurers competing for clientele. The government would regulate the insurance companies to manage costs. The legislation was very complex, spanning more than 1,400 pages. The support for the legislation was mixed, despite having a Democratic majority in both the House and the Senate. In addition, there was opposition from the National Federation of Independent Businesses who feared that mandating insurance would strain small businesses. Ultimately, the legislation failed to pass.

Development of the PPACA

The next legislation to be proposed that concerned nationalized health insurance was the PPACA. The PPACA was introduced to the House of Representatives on September 17, 2009, as the "Service Members Home Ownership Tax Act of 2009" (H.R. 3590) proposed by Representative Charles Rangler, a Democrat from New York. It was passed in the House on October 8, 2009, and sent to the Senate for approval. The Senate, in typical fashion, retitled the bill and replaced a majority of the text in their amendments. The modified version passed the Senate vote on December 24, 2009, with all 60 members of the Democratic Party voting in favor and all 40 members of the Republican Party voting against the legislation. At this point, the legislation returned to the House of Representatives for approval of the amendments. The Speaker of the House, Nancy Pelosi, held the bill for 3 months in an attempt to win enough votes for the passage of the legislation. On March 21, 2010, the House passed HR3590 by a narrow margin with 219 Democrats voting for its passage and 212 bipartisan representatives voting against its passage. President Barak Obama signed the bill into law on March 23, 2010. The legislation was then amended under the Health Care and Education Reconciliation Act (HCERA), which was passed on March 30, 2010. The finalized legislation addresses several areas of health care, some of which will be addressed in the next section.

Timeline for Implementation

The PPACA is an extremely complex piece of legislation addressing 89 different areas (THJKFF, 2010b). Due to the complex nature of this legislation, only those areas that address prevention will be discussed. These areas are also in line with the amendments to the PPACA caused by the passage of the HCERA.

2010: Prevention and Public Health Funds

The PPACA appropriated $5 billion for every fiscal year from 2010 until 2014 and $2 billion for each subsequent year to be allocated toward prevention and public health programs. The DHHS allocated $500 million from the Prevention and Public Health Fund for the fiscal year 2010. Half of this funding was dedicated to improving the supply of primary care providers, and the other half was used to support public health and prevention priorities. In February 2011, DHHS announced that it was using $750 million of the funds to help prevention efforts in areas such as tobacco use.

New Prevention Council

In July 2010, President Obama signed an Executive Order creating the National Prevention, Health Promotion and Public Health Council. The council, headed by the surgeon general, was ordered to develop a national prevention, health promotion, and public health strategy. In June 2011, the Council released the National Prevention Strategy, which touches on all areas of health, both physical and mental. Included among the priorities are "tobacco free living," "preventing drug abuse and excessive alcohol use," and "mental and emotional well-being" (National Prevention, Health Promotion and Public Health Council, 2011, p. 5).

Coverage of Preventative Benefits

For all health insurance policies beginning on or after September 23, 2010, coverage of preventative benefits that were deemed as important by the Preventative Services Task Force was mandated to be provided at a minimum coverage without cost sharing.

2011: Medicare Preventative Benefits

Implemented on January 1, 2011, this aspect of the legislation authorizes Medicare coverage for a personalized prevention plan, which includes a comprehensive health risk assessment. In addition, it eliminates co-pays for recommended Medicare-covered preventative services. Regrettably, the only area of mental illness prevention that this part of the legislation addresses is tobacco cessation (USDHHS, Centers for Medicare and Medicaid Services, 2011).

Chronic Disease Prevention in Medicaid

In February 2011, the Centers for Medicare and Medicaid Services announced that they were making $100 million in grants available for states to offer Medicaid enrollees with incentives to participate in prevention programs and meet specific health behavior targets.

Wellness Program Grants

This portion of the legislation provides grants, lasting up to 5 years, for small employers to establish wellness programs for employees.

2013: Medicaid Coverage of Preventative Services

This element of the legislation provides states with a 1% point increase in federal matching payments for states that provide recommended preventative services to Medicaid clients with no co-pays.

2014: Wellness Programs Mandated in Insurance

This portion of the legislation mandates that insurance companies incorporate wellness and preventative services coverage by January 1, 2014. Employees that participate in the wellness programs and reach specified health-related standards may receive rewards of up to 30% to 50% off the cost of coverage. In addition to employer coverage, this aspect of the legislation establishes 10 pilot programs for states to implement similar rewards programs. Mental health standards and services are incorporated within this element of the legislation.

Discussion Questions

1. Mental health services were largely neglected in the PPACA. What services do you think should have been included? How do you think that these services could have been better addressed through nationalized health insurance legislation?

2. What do you think are the criteria for elements that are included or not included into the legislation? How can you as a mental health professional work within these guidelines?

5 Changing Public Policies

Public policy is a very broad term. It encompasses legislation, regulations, rules, and managerial practices at the international, federal, state, and local levels and for issues like human trafficking, human subjects' protections, global warming, or trade. International agreements have been important in the fields of prevention and mental health. Take, for example, the Nuremberg Code, written in 1947 in response to the abuses that happened in concentration camps during World War II. The Nuremberg Code established ethical principles around human experimentation. In conjunction with the Declaration of Helsinki, the Nuremberg Code serves as the basis of the Code of Regulations issued by the USDHHS, which governs federally funded research in the United States. On a global scale, the Nuremberg Code has influenced human rights law. Informed consent by subjects in human studies is now included as Article 7 of the United Nations International Covenant on Civil and Political Rights and serves as the basis of the International Ethical Guidelines for Biomedical Research Involving Human Subjects, guidelines set up by the World Health Organization (Shuster, 1997).

In the international arena, the World Federation for Mental Health serves as a global advocacy and public education organization. Their mission is to "promote the advancement of mental health awareness, prevention of mental disorders, advocacy, and best practice recovery focused interventions worldwide" (see www.wfmh.org). The World Health Organization also takes a leadership role for the 192 member states of the United Nations by shaping their research agenda, setting norms and standards, and providing policy options, among other responsibilities (see www.who.int). While there are many other worthy organizations that deal with prevention such as the Bill and Melinda Gates Foundation, this chapter focuses on a number of the mechanisms that have led to public policy development, primarily in the United States, and tries to provide some guidance for practicing psychologists and other like-minded individuals who want to influence public policies. What follows are eight success stories where public policies were changed followed by the lessons that can be learned from them.

Examples 1 and 2: Whistleblowers and the Role of the Media

The Tuskegee Syphilis Study

Media exposés can provoke changes in public policy. For example, between 1932 and 1972, the U.S. Public Health Service studied the progression of syphilis among 600 poor, black, rural men in Tuskegee, Alabama. Effective treatment was withheld even after the penicillin was deemed an effective cure for syphilis in the 1940s, and the scientists actively prevented some participants from accessing treatments. Some victims of the study died, some wives of these men contracted syphilis, and some children of these men were born with congenital syphilis. The story was printed in the *Washington Star* on July 25, 1972, and was front-page news in *The New York Times* the next day. Following the exposé, Senator Edward Kennedy called for Congressional hearings that led to the National Research Act of 1974, creating the National Commission for the Protection of Human Subjects. (For a review of events leading to this act, see Blustein, 2005.)

The Willowbrook Hepatitis Study

Similarly, children with mental disabilities were injected with the virus that causes hepatitis A at the Willowbrook School in Staten Island in New York. This study was approved and funded by the Armed Services Epidemiological Board and similarly approved by the executive faculty of the New York University School of Medicine. This research took place between 1963 and 1966. Its purpose was to determine if gamma globulin was an effective treatment for hepatitis A.

The school housed 6,000 children in 1965, although it had a maximum capacity of 4,000. Often parents consented to have their children participate in the study because it assured admission into the overcrowded facility (DuBois, 2004). However, the parental consent letter minimized the potential risks to the children.

An advocate for mentally disabled children gained access to the school posing as a social worker and shared her observations with the press (Robinson & Unruh, 2008). The media kept the Willowbrook School in the press and a class-action lawsuit was filed in 1972, which was settled 3 years later. The media attention around the situation and lawsuit led in large part to the passage of the Civil Rights of Institutionalized Persons Act (CRIPA) of 1980. CRIPA gives the U.S. Attorney General the responsibility of investigating institutional conditions and filing lawsuits if there is a pattern or practice of unlawful conditions (see U.S. Department of Justice at http://www.justice.gov/crt/about/spl/cripa.php).

Fortunately, not all motivations for change in the public policy sphere are as notorious as Tuskegee or Willowbrook. However, in both of these cases, the press played an important role in bringing information about deplorable and unethical treatment of individuals to the public's eye.

Examples 3 to 8: Personal Stories

Mental Health America

In 1900, a graduate of Yale University named Clifford Beers was institutionalized in Connecticut mental health facilities after a breakdown in the aftermath of his brother's death. Beers spent several years hospitalized in a number of facilities and suffered horrible treatment, including mental and physical abuse. In 1908, Beers published his autobiography, *A Mind That Found Itself*, documenting his illness and the state of mental health care in the United States. The book was influential in its call for reforms in the treatment of the mentally ill. In the same year, Beers established the Connecticut Society for Mental Hygiene, which 1 year later expanded to the National Committee for Mental Hygiene. In 1950, the National Committee merged with two other organizations to form the National Association of Mental Health (NAMH).

The NAMH has had an activist agenda, participating in the 1960s on the Congress' Joint Commission on Mental Illness and Mental Health. In 1970, NAMH became the National Mental Health Association (NMHA), which was instrumental in the development and passage of the 1980 Mental Health Systems Act. This activist agenda includes the establishment of commissions on the mental health of the unemployed and homeless, the insanity defense, as well as the shaping of the Americans with Disabilities Act (ADA) of 1990 and the Mental Health Parity Act of 1996. In 2006, NMHA became Mental Health America, and it continues its activist agenda on behalf of the rights of those individuals with mental illnesses.

Amber Alerts

Amber Hagerman was abducted while bicycling on her block in Arlington, Texas, on January 13, 1996. A neighbor heard her scream and saw a man take Amber and drive off. It took 8 minutes from the time Amber rode away on her bicycle from her home until a call was placed to 911. Four days later Amber's body was found in a drainage ditch in Arlington. Her throat had been slit.

In the aftermath of the murder, Richard Hagerman and Amber's mother, Donna Whitson, established People Against Sex Offenders (PASO). They circulated petitions to encourage Texas legislators into passing stronger laws to protect children. PASO received considerable media attention, and eventually, a concerned citizen raised the question about how the police and media might use the radio Emergency Alert System to inform the public of child abductions with the same urgency of weather emergencies such as tornadoes or hurricanes. A Dallas Amber Plan was initiated in July of 1997, which resulted in the safe return of a child just 16 months later. Houston set up an Amber Plan in 2000, and in 2002 the program went statewide. The loss of Amber Hagerman eventually resulted in the America's Missing: Broadcasting Emergency Response (AMBER) alert system that now operates in all states. Alerts of suspected abductions are broadcasted on regular and cable television stations, commercial and satellite radio stations, the Emergency Alert System, and the National Oceanic and Atmospheric Administration (NOAA) weather radio. Bulletins are also sent via e-mail, SMS text messages, and electronic traffic signs, as well as via LED/LCD billboards at various private companies. The National Center for Missing and Exploited Children (www.missingkids.com) is credited with successfully recovering 540 children as of May 2011.

Garrett Lee Smith Memorial Act

On September 8, 2003, Garrett Lee Smith committed suicide. Garrett was the son of U.S. Senator Gordon H. Smith. On October 24, 2004, a bipartisan, bicameral Congress passed the Garrett Lee Smith Memorial Act (GLSMA), which created three suicide prevention programs targeted at youth. One program provides grants to states and tribal organizations to develop and operate state or tribal suicide prevention plans. The second program provides funding to colleges and universities for suicide education, intervention, and referral teams. The third program established a national resource center, which was tasked with collecting, analyzing, and disseminating information on best practices in suicide prevention. The DHHS budgeted $54 million for GLSMA in 2011 (USDHHS, 2011).

Insanity Defense Reform Act of 1984

John Hinkley Jr. attempted to assassinate President Ronald Reagan on March 30, 1981. As President Reagan was leaving a speaking engagement at the Washington Hilton, Hinkley fired a revolver six times hitting Press Secretary James Brady, a D.C. police officer, and a Secret Service agent. The sixth bullet ricocheted off the armored limousine hitting President Reagan who had been pushed by a secret service agent into the vehicle. The President's lung had been punctured, but quick action on the part of the secret service and medical community led to his quick recovery. The assassination attempt was caught on video and replayed by the media again and again. There was no doubt that the shooter was John Hinkley Jr.

On June 21, 1982, Hinkley was found not guilty by reason of insanity. Interestingly, he was confined at St. Elizabeth's, the first large-scale, federally operated psychiatric hospital founded by Congress in 1952, in large part due to the lobbying efforts of Dorothea Dix, an advocate for the mentally ill. The public was outraged, and the verdict led many states to change their insanity defense laws (Hans & Slater, 1983), and at the national level, it led to the Insanity Defense Reform Act of 1984. The act codified at 18 U.S.C. § 17 states,

> It is an affirmative defense to a prosecution under any Federal statute that, at the time of the commission of the acts constituting the offense, the defendant, as a result of a severe mental disease or defect, was unable to appreciate the nature and quality of the wrongfulness of his acts. Mental disease or defect does not otherwise constitute a defense.

The act eliminated the Irresistible Impulse Test from an insanity plea and additionally requires that the defendant "has the burden of proving the defense of insanity by clear and convincing evidence."

Brady Handgun Violence Prevention Act of 1993

The Gun Control Act of 1968 was passed in response to the assassinations of prominent individuals in the 1960s, including President John F. Kennedy, Dr. Martin Luther King Jr., and Senator Robert F. Kennedy. This act identified categories of individuals that were too high risk to own guns, including, among others, felons and the mentally ill. However, high-risk individuals could still falsify information and purchase guns as gun sales were operated on an honor system. Subsequent to the assassination attempt on President Reagan in which Press Secretary James Brady sustained serious head injuries, he and his wife, Sarah, began a 7-year campaign for gun control. In 1993, the Brady Handgun Violence Prevention Act required background checks for individuals purchasing firearms. Provided that the state has no additional requirements, a firearm can be transferred to a purchaser subsequent to approval from the FBI's National Instant Criminal Background Check System. According to the Brady Campaign to Prevent Gun Violence (http://www.bradycampaign.org/legislation/backgroundchecks/bradylaw), this law has successfully blocked 1.9 million purchase attempts by high-risk individuals from gun dealers.

Ryan White CARE Act

Ryan White was diagnosed with AIDS at age 13 from a contaminated blood transfusion to treat his hemophilia. He was one of the first children and first hemophiliacs diagnosed with AIDS. As a student in Western Heights Middle School in Russiaville, Indiana, he was expelled because AIDS was not well understood at the time, even though doctors indicated that he posed no threat to other students. A protracted lawsuit ensued with the school district, and the media attention transformed Ryan into a celebrity and poster child for AIDS. The U.S. District Court in Indianapolis eventually overturned the school ban, but Ryan and his family ultimately moved to Cicero, after a gun was fired into their home and after Ryan's unhappy return to Western Heights, where parents and teachers signed petitions and even held fund-raisers to try and prevent him from returning to school. Ryan was welcomed at Hamilton Heights High School in Cicero.

Ryan and his family felt strongly about the importance of education about HIV/AIDS. He appeared frequently in the newspapers, television, and at fund-raisers with national figures such as President Ronald Reagan and Nancy Reagan and Surgeon General C. Everett Koop as well as celebrities such as Michael Jackson and Elton John, who sang at his funeral. (For more details on Ryan White, see the DHHS website at http://hab.hrsa.gov/abouthab/index.html or the White House website at http://www.whitehouse.gov/blog/2009/10/30/honoring-legacy-ryan-white.)

Four months after his death, the Ryan White Comprehensive AIDS Resources Emergency (CARE) Act was passed in August of 1990. The Ryan White CARE fund serves as the "payer of the last resort" when no other means of support are available for to support treatment for low-income individuals who are uninsured or underinsured and their families. There are five funding streams under this act that serve to fund (1) areas with a high prevalence of the disease, (2) states, (3) primary health care for those with HIV, (4) family-centered care, and (5) some specialized programming. The CARE fund is currently funded at $2.1 billion.

Changing Public Policy: Lessons Learned

The eight successful examples of policy change detailed above describe situations that existed, sometimes for long periods of time, before any changes took place. What was it about these untimely deaths, assassination attempts, or mistreatment at the hands of mental health care professionals that triggered new policies and legislation?

First, in each of the examples above, attention was drawn to a particular problem because of widespread media coverage, or in the case of Clifford Beers, the publication of his book. This attention created a window of opportunity for change even though the underlying problems had existed, sometimes for decades. Key stakeholders and the media had shaped the policy issues in ways that were understandable. Key legislators and policy makers could relate to the issues. In fact, several victims were political figures. Even though there were individuals and lobbying groups who opposed change and wanted to preserve the status quo, the tide of sentiment pushed the policy agenda forward. One take-away message is that you can *take advantage of windows of opportunity to advance change.*

Another observation about these examples is that you can *use the media to help advance change*. In each of the above examples, media coverage was widespread, although not always initiated by long-time, committed activists. Ryan White was a public figure and appeared in the media with presidents, sports figures, government officials, and high-profile entertainers. Media exposés created the turmoil around the Tuskegee and Willowbrook studies. The repeated viewing of the assassination attempt on President Reagan and the highly publicized acquittal of his shooter by reason of insanity helped create circumstances to change laws relating to the insanity defense and later, the more controversial gun control legislation. The Amber Hagerman abduction and murder were front-page news. If you decide to work with the media, bear in mind that they can change messages in ways you do not intend and that sometimes "going public" can break the trust you may have established with key stakeholders.

If you want to get your issues aired, but don't want to go directly to the media, set up a blog, website, or tweet. Technologies are changing, and particularly, younger citizens are increasingly comfortable with them. There are blogs on nearly every conceivable policy issue from health care to taxes to foreign policy.

Change Does Not Come Without Effort, Sometimes Years of Effort

The Brady family formed the Brady Campaign to Stop Handgun Violence, and it took 6 years before the Brady Handgun Violence Prevention Act was enacted. The Hagerman family established PASO and kept the search for their child's abductor in the news. Amber was murdered in 1996. It was not until 2003 that the Prosecutorial Remedies and Other Tools to end the Exploitation of Children Today Act codified the National AMBER Alert Coordinator role in the Department of Justice. If you want to change public policy, it may take serious dedication over a long period of time.

Building or Joining an Advocacy Group Can Help

Clifford Beers established a society to advocate for the rights and reasonable treatment of the mentally ill, an institution that still operates today. The Hagerman family established PASO. The Brady family formed the Brady Campaign to Stop Handgun Violence. But you do not need to start your own group. There are numerous local grassroots organizations that fight for change that you can join. At the national level, a smaller number of larger advocacy groups lobby for changes in legislation and enhanced funding for mental health and prevention programming. Some examples include the American Psychological Association, the American Mental

Health Counselors Association, the American School Counselor Association, the National Council for Community Behavioral Healthcare (for health care organizations), Mental Health America, and the National Alliance on Mental Illness.

Also bear in mind that many privately initiated nongovernmental groups have had significant effects on private practice as opposed to public policy. The Alcoholics, Narcotics, Gamblers, and Overeaters Anonymous groups have had profound effects on the lives of many citizens. Alcoholics Anonymous alone estimates its global membership at 2.2 million (www.aa .org). The story of the difficult beginnings of Alcoholics Anonymous as written by Bill W. (1996) can be found in Chapter 1 of *The A.A. Service Manual*. Narcotics Anonymous does not provide membership numbers, but as of 2007, it had more than 25,065 groups holding more than 43,900 weekly meetings in 127 countries (see www.na.org).

Another lesson learned is that *whistle-blowing can work*. In collaboration with the media, whistle-blowing can focus attention on serious problems. This was clearly the case for both the Tuskegee and Willowbrook studies. However, whistle-blowing can have serious ramifications for the whistle-blower, including loss of job, incarceration, and lawsuits. Especially, if you are a federal employee and you plan to blow the whistle, check the National Whistleblowers Center website (www.whistleblowers.org) to find out about your legal protections.

While it is less obvious from the above examples, another lesson learned about changing federal policies is to *know your legislators*. Some of them have personal stories that will make them more receptive to your concerns. For example, Senator Edward Kennedy had a mentally handicapped sister and was a known advocate for policies for the handicapped. He was also a sponsor of the Civil Rights Commission Rights Amendments to protect people from discrimination because of their disabilities. Additionally, among others, he cosponsored the Americans with Disabilities Act of 1990, the Education for All Handicapped Children Act of 1975, the Handicapped Children's Protection Act of 1986, and the Economic Opportunities for Disabled Americans Act of 1986.

In 1968, Shirley Chisholm was the first African American woman elected to Congress. Chisholm represented New York's 12th District and was interested in helping the urban, poor people. However, due to pressure from southern Congressional members, Ms. Chisholm was assigned membership on the House's Agricultural Committee. Ms. Chisholm, unhappy with her assignment, spoke with Rabbi Schneerson of her district who suggested that she pay attention to the hungry. Ms. Chisholm focused her attention of U.S. food surpluses and was instrumental in expanding access to the Food Stamps program, now renamed the Supplemental Nutritional Assistance Program (SNAP), and the food education and supplementation program for low-income pregnant and nursing women and their infants and children under the age of 5, the WIC program. In fiscal year (FY) 2010, SNAP served 40.3 million

Americans with expenditures of $68.3 billion, while the WIC program had 9.1 million participants and expenditures of $6.7 billion (U.S. Department of Agriculture, 2011).

Most Policy Changes Are Incremental

The examples of policy changes discussed above all involve large changes to federal policy stimulated by whistle-blowing or personal tragedies that received substantial media coverage. Most policy changes do not take place in these ways. Most change is on a smaller scale, is less dramatic, and more incremental. Changes in eligibility rules for social programs or funding formulas at all levels of government are common occurrences. While they do not have the visibility of new national legislation, they can be equally important in the lives of citizens.

There are notable cases in which policy analysis research has been instrumental in changing public policies. For example, in 1984, Lawrence W. Sherman and Richard A. Berk published an article, "The Specific Deterrent Effects of Arrest for Domestic Assault." At that time, many police officers either delayed or did not respond to calls of domestic violence for a variety of reasons. It was dangerous duty and charges against the assailant were frequently dropped. Some considered domestic violence a family, not public, issue (Hoctor, 1997). In collaboration with the Minneapolis Police Department, Sherman and Berk conducted a field experiment. Three police responses to simple assault were randomly assigned to domestic violence suspects: (1) an arrest, (2) informal advice, or (3) an order for the suspect to leave the premises for 8 hours. Both official records and victim reports indicated that the arrested suspects manifested less subsequent violence than those who had been advised or those who left the premises.

The study received prime-time news coverage, and the results were reported in *The New York Times*. Despite the authors' cautions that the study should be replicated, many U.S. policy departments adopted mandatory arrest policies in domestic violence cases. The 1984 U.S. Attorney General's Task Force on Family Violence relied extensively on the study's findings in recommending that a criminal justice approach be used in these cases (Gelles, 1993). By 1989, 84% of urban police agencies reported having either mandatory or pro-arrest policies in domestic battery cases (Hoctor, 1997). Within 8 years of the study's release, 15 states and the District of Columbia moved legislation to mandate police arrests in all probable cause cases of domestic violence (Schmidt & Sherman, 1993). Since the original study has been published, a number of other researchers have replicated the experiment (sometimes with new policy options) in different locations, and the results have been mixed. Public sentiment and public policy regarding arrest in domestic violence cases has not changed.

In contrast, in 2008, Trenholm et al. published a study, "Impacts of the Abstinence Education on Teen Sexual Activity, Risk of Pregnancy, and Risk of Sexually Transmitted Diseases" in the *Journal of Policy Analysis and Management*. The study received the American Evaluation Association's Outstanding Evaluation Award in 2009. This randomized experiment found that abstinence-only sex education had no significant impact on the sexual activity of teens or in rates of unprotected sex. The study was described in news and opinion pieces in *The New York Times* (April 28, 2007), *The Washington Post*, *USA Today*, NPR, BBC, and ABC News (Brandon, Smith, Trenholm, & Devaney, 2010). The results of the study took place in a highly charged political environment and were at odds with the views of President G. W. Bush and his administration that had been strong supporters of abstinence-only sex education (Lewin, 2010). Shortly after the study's release, the government cancelled a request for proposal (RFP) for a follow-up study, but did issue a new RFP months later. While the new RFP did take into consideration the study findings and increases the ages at which abstinence-only education was studied, support of abstinence-only sex education did not diminish for the duration of the Bush presidency. President Obama's administration, however, has moved toward more comprehensive sex education.

It is interesting to compare these two studies because they both tackled large and important problems. Both used sound, state-of-the-art methodologies. Both were well documented and had substantial media coverage. Why then did the domestic violence study gain political traction, while the abstinence-only sex education study had minimal impact on policy for the remainder of the Bush presidency? It is likely that there is little political opposition to arresting wife beaters, whereas sex education for adolescents treads on some firmly held religious beliefs about what does and does not constitute appropriate behavior.

Rigorous, sound public policy research seems to have more political sway when there are no political or religious controversies surrounding the issue (e.g., abortion, stem cell research, teaching evolution, the hand-up not a handout debate in the 1996 welfare reform legislation). For example, for a variety of reasons, most politicians support the U.S. Child Support Enforcement (CSE) program. The program secures child support from the noncustodial parent and transfers it to the custodial parent on behalf of the child. In cases of joint custody, the financial transfer equalizes the incomes of the two households. The program is good for children and also helps ensure that parents, not taxpayers, support their children. The program had a caseload of 15.7 million and collected nearly $26.6 billion in FY 2008 (USDHHS, Office of Child Support Enforcement, 2010).

More than many government agencies, the federal CSE office has strong relationships with the research community. For example, in the late 1980s, the State of Washington greatly expanded and studied the effects of its in-hospital paternity establishment program. The program was recognized as a best practice, and with the Omnibus Budget Reconciliation Act of 1993,

Congress mandated that all states implement an in-hospital paternity establishment program based on the Washington state model (State of Washington, Department of Social and Health Services, 2006). Demonstration projects, state innovation grants, and research on child support have played pivotal roles in the use and development of child support guidelines, use of automatic wage withholding, use of electronic technologies to transfer child support to custodial parents, and more. The National Child Support Enforcement Association has a research track at their national conferences, a research committee that screens new research for policy-relevant work that is disseminated on their website and in their newsletter.

And, there are other venues for policy research to enter timely political debates. The U.S. Congressional Research Service uses current research to prepare reports for members of Congress and their staff. State legislative research offices use policy research, as do state-level departments. As a researcher, it is important to build a relationship of trust with state officials. Many politicians view research as cudgels that can be used against them in campaigns. It can take years to establish good working relationships with your state administrators and politicians.

Other Avenues to Influence Public Policy

Although it seems obvious, you can run for political office, volunteer, or get appointed to a board or commission; you can serve as a campaign director, work as a lobbyist, or work as a grassroots organizer; you can circulate petitions, hold sit-ins, or march for progress. Again, you can use the media to get your message out. Define the problem clearly, support your position with evidence, and propose a solution.

You can inform policy makers and the legal profession by teaching classes for continuing legal studies credits. In controversial cases that have the potential to change public policy, you can serve as an expert witness. If you are an academic, you can conduct well-designed research studies on the policy area you want to influence irrespective of whether it is on alcohol, tobacco, drug addiction, or a myriad other mental health and prevention topics. Do not let your work languish in a scholarly journal. Use your university's media relations to highlight your work or write op-ed pieces. Use electronic media. One final note, in any and all approaches, it is best to present a balanced perspective. Be realistic about the financial circumstances of the organization in which you would like to create change.

References _____

American Council for Drug Education. (1999). *Basic facts about drugs: Tobacco.* Retrieved from http://www.acde.org/common/Tobacco.htm

American Lung Association. (2010). *State of tobacco control 2010.* Retrieved from http://www.stateoftobaccocontrol.org/state-grades/state-rankings/smokefree-air-laws.html

American Psychiatric Association. (2000). *Diagnostic and statistical manual of mental disorders* (4th ed., text revision). Washington, DC: Author.

American School Counselors Association. (2010). Retrieved from http://www.schoolcounselor.org/

Anderson, R. N., & Smith, B. L. (2003). *Deaths: Leading causes for 2001. National Vital Statistics Report* (Vol. 52). Hyattsville, MD: National Center for Health Statistics.

Andrews, D. A., Zinger, I., Hoge, R. D., Bonta, J., Gendreau, P., & Cullen, F. T. (1990). Does correctional treatment work? A clinically relevant and psychologically informed meta-analysis. *Criminology, 28*(3), 369–404.

Arthur, M. W., Hawkins, J. D., Pollard, J. A., Catalano, R. F., & Baglioni, A. J., Jr. (2002). Measuring risk and protective factors for use, delinquency, and other adolescent problem behaviors: Communities that care youth survey. *Evaluation Review, 26*(6), 575–601.

Associated Press. (2005, October 29). *Schools D.A.R.E. to get real.* Retrieved from http://cannabisnews.com/news/14/thread14588.shtml

Bardach, E. (2005). *A practical guide for policy analysis: The eightfold path to more effective problem solving.* Washington, DC: Congressional Quarterly Press.

Beautrais, A. (2007). Suicide by jumping: A review of research and prevention strategies. *Crisis: Journal of Crisis Intervention and Suicide Prevention, 28,* 58–63.

Beers, C. (1908). *A Mind that found itself: An autobiography.* Pittsburgh, PA: University of Pittsburgh Press.

Berman, G., & Fox, A. (2009). *Lessons from the battle over D.A.R.E.: The complicated relationship between research and practice.* Washington, DC: Government Printing Office.

Beyers, J. M., Toumbourou, J. W., Catalano, R., Arthur, M. W., & Hawkins, J. D. (2004). A cross-national comparison of risk and protective factors for adolescent substance use: The United States and Australia. *Journal of Adolescent Health, 35,* 3–16.

Birkeland, S., Murphy-Graham, E., & Weiss, C. (2005). Good reasons for ignoring good evaluation: The case of the drug abuse resistance education (D.A.R.E.) program. *Evaluation and Program Planning, 28,* 247–256.

Blaustein, M., & Flemming, A. (2009). Suicide from the Golden Gate Bridge. *American Journal of Psychiatry, 166,* 1111–1116.

Blustein, J. (2005). Toward a more public discussion of the ethics of federal social program evaluation. *Journal of Policy Analysis and Management, 24,* 824–846.

Board of Directors. (2005, April 22). *Approve adoption of new policy-level criteria for use in evaluating physical suicide deterrent systems* (Golden Gate Bridge, Highway and Transportation District Resolution No. 2005-033). San Francisco, CA: Author. Retrieved from http://www.goldengatebridge.org/projects/documents/Res_2005-033_SuicDetCriteria.pdf

Brandon, P. R., Smith, N. L., Trenholm, C., & Devaney, B. (2010). Evaluation exemplar: The critical importance of stakeholder relations in a national experimental abstinence education evaluation. *American Journal of Evaluation, 31,* 517–531. Retrieved from http://aje.sagepub.com/content/31/4/517

Broderick, P. C., & Blewitt, P. A. (2010). *The life span: Human development for helping professionals* (3rd ed.). Upper Saddle River, NJ: Pearson Education.

Brown, A. S., & Susser, E. S. (2008). Prenatal nutritional deficiency and risk of adult schizophrenia. *Schizophrenia Bulletin, 34*(6), 1054–1063.

Bureau of Justice Assistance. (1991). *An introduction to DARE; Drug Abuse Resistance Education, program brief* (2nd ed.). Washington, DC: Government Printing Office.

Bureau of Justice Statistics. (2011). *Recidivism.* Retrieved from, http://bjs.ojp.usdoj.gov/index.cfm?ty=tp&tid=17

Carey, B. (2009, November 26). Brain surgery for mental illness offers hope and risk. *The New York Times.* Retrieved from http://www.nytimes.com/2009/11/27/health/research/27brain.html?adxnnl=1&adxnnlx=1313174413-ui/twLD4VlY/BY8PBEUjQg

Catalano, R. F., Haggerty, K. P., Hawkins, J. D., & Elgin, J. (2011). Prevention of substance use and substance use disorders: The role of risk and protective factors. In Y. Kaminer & K. C. Winters (Eds.), *Clinical manual of adolescent substance abuse treatment* (pp. 25–63). Washington, DC: American Psychiatric Publishing.

Centers for Disease Control. (2007). *Eliminating disparities in mental health.* Retrieved from http://www.cdc.gov/omhd/AMH/factsheets/mental.htm

Chadha-Hooks, P. L., Park, J. H., Hilty, D. M., & Seritan, A. L. (2010). Postpartum depression: An original survey of screening practices within a healthcare system. *Journal of Psychosomatic Obstetrics & Gynecology, 31*(3), 199–205.

Clayton, R. C., Cattarello, A., & Walden, K. P. (1991). Sensation seeking as a potential mediating variable for school-based prevention intervention: A two-year follow-up of DARE. *Health Communication, 3,* 229–239.

Coles, C. (1994). Critical periods for prenatal alcohol exposure: Evidence from animal and human studies. *Journal of the National Institute on Alcohol Abuse and Alcoholism, Alcohol Health and Research World, 18,* 22–29.

Compton, W. M., Conway, K. P., Stinson, F. S., & Grant, B. F. (2006). Changes in the prevalence of major depression and comorbid substance use disorders in the United States between 1991–1992 and 2001–2002. *American Journal of Psychiatry, 163*(12), 2141–2147.

Conner, C. D. (2009). *American lung association celebrates public health victory.* Retrieved from http://www.lungusa.org/press-room/press-releases/public-health-victory.html

Council for Accreditation of Counseling and Related Educational Programs. (2009). *2009 standards*. Retrieved from http://www.cacrep.org/doc/2009%20Standards%20with%20cover.pdf

Cox, D. W., Ghahramanlou-Holloway, M., Szeto, E. H., Greene, F. N., Engel, C., Wynn, G. H., . . . Grammer, G. (2011). Gender differences on documented trauma histories: Inpatients admitted to a military psychiatric unit for suicide related thoughts or behaviors. *Journal of Nervous and Mental Disease, 199*(3), 183–190.

Cummins, S. E., Bailey, L., Campbell, S., Koon-Kirby, C., & Zhu, S. (2007). Tobacco cessation quitlines in North America: A descriptive study. *Tobacco Control, 16*(Suppl. 1), i9–i15.

Dakof, G. A., Cohen, J. B., Henderson, C. E., Duarte, E., Boustani, M., Blackburn, A., . . . Hawes, S. (2010). A randomized pilot study of the engaging moms program for family drug court. *Journal of Substance Abuse Treatment, 38*(3), 263–274.

DeJong, W. (1987). A short-term evaluation of Project DARE (Drug Abuse Resistance Education): Preliminary indications of effectiveness. *Journal of Drug Education, 17*, 279–294.

Department of Defense. (2011). *Real warriors, real battles, real strength*. Retrieved from http://www.realwarriors.net/

Department of Education. (2002). *Exemplary and promising safe, disciplined, and drug-free schools programs 2001*. Washington, DC: Government printing office.

Department of Transportation, National Highway Traffic Safety Administration. (2010). *Traffic safety facts 2009: A compilation of motor vehicle crash data from the Fatality Analysis Reporting System and the General Estimates System* (DOT HS 811 402). Washington, DC: Government Printing Office.

Department of Veterans Affairs, Office of Inspector General. (2007). *Healthcare inspection: Implementing VHA's mental health strategic plan initiatives for suicide prevention*. (Report No. 06-03706-126). Washington, DC: Government Printing Office.

Drug Abuse Resistance Education. (2009). *D.A.R.E. 2009 annual report*. Retrieved from http://dare-america.org/home/documents/0310DARE_AnnualReport_11WEB_000.pdf

Drug Abuse Resistance Education. (2011). *D.A.R.E. official website*. Retrieved from http://www.dare.org

DuBois, J. M. (2004). Hepatitis studies at the Willowbrook State School for Children with Mental Retardation. *Ethics in Mental Health Research*. Retrieved from http://ethics.iit.edu/eelibrary/node/2617

Elder, R. W., Lawrence, B., Ferguson, A., Naimi, T. S., Brewer, R. D., Chattopadhyay, S. K., . . . Fielding, J. E., the Task Force on Community Prevention Services. (2010). The effectiveness of tax policy interventions for reducing excessive alcohol consumptions and related harms. *American Journal of Preventative Medicine, 38*(2), 217–222.

Ennett, S. T., Tobler, N. S., Ringwalt, C. L., & Flewelling, R. L. (1994). How effective is drug abuse resistance education? A meta-analysis of Project DARE outcome evaluations. *American Journal of Public Health, 84*(9), 1394–1401.

Feldman, R. D. (2000). *American health care: Government, market processes, and the public interest*. Oakland, CA: Independent Institute.

Florida Suicide Prevention Coalition. (2011). *State history*. Retrieved from http://www.floridasuicideprevention.org/state_history.htm

Fornili, K., & Burda, C. (2010). Overview of current federal policy for substance use disorders. *Journal of Addictions Nursing, 21*(4), 247–251.

Gelles, R. J. (1993). Constraints against family violence: How well do they work? *American Behavioral Scientist, 36,* 575–587.

Gjerdingen, D. K., & Yawn, B. P. (2007). Postpartum depression screening: Importance, methods, barriers and recommendations for practice. *Journal of the American Board of Family Medicine, 20*(3), 280–288.

Gonda, X., Fountoulakis, K. N., Kaprinis, G., & Rihmer, Z. (2007). Prediction and prevention of suicide in patients with unipolar depression and anxiety. *Annals of General Psychiatry, 6*(23), 1–8.

Hans, V. P., & Slater, D. (1983). John Hinkley, Jr. and the insanity defense: The public's verdict. *Public Opinion Quarterly, 47,* 202–212.

Harley, M., Kelleher, I., Clarke, M., Lynch, F., Arseneault, L., Connor, D., . . . Cannon, M. (2010). Cannabis use and childhood trauma interact additively to increase the risk of psychotic symptoms in adolescence. *Psychological medicine: A Journal of Research in Psychiatry and the Allied Sciences, 40*(10), 1627–1634.

Harry S. Truman Library and Museum. (2011). President Truman's proposed health program. Retrieved from http://www.trumanlibrary.org/anniversaries/health-program.htm

Hasin, D. S., Goodwin, R. D., Stinson, F. S., & Grant, B. F. (2005). Epidemiology of major depressive disorder. *Archives of General Psychiatry, 62,* 1097–1106.

Hawkins, J. D., Graham, J. W., Maguin, E., Abbott, R., Hill, K. G., & Catalano, R. F. (1997). Exploring the effects of age of alcohol use initiation and psychosocial risk factors on subsequent alcohol misuse. *Journal of Studies on Alcohol, 58*(3), 280–290.

The Henry J. Kaiser Family Foundation. (2009, March). *National health insurance: A brief history of reform efforts in the U.S.* Retrieved from http://www.kff.org/healthreform/upload/7871.pdf

The Henry J. Kaiser Family Foundation. (2010a). *Focus on health reform: Summary of new health reform law.* Retrieved from http://www.kff.org/healthreform/upload/8061.pdf

The Henry J. Kaiser Family Foundation. (2010b). *Implementation timeline.* Retrieved from http://healthreform.kff.org/Timeline.aspx

Hiday, V. A., & Ray, B. (2010). Arrests two years after exiting a well-established mental health court. *Psychiatric Services, 61*(5), 463–468.

Hoctor, M. (1997). Domestic violence as a crime against the state: The need for mandatory arrest in California. *California Law Review, 85,* 643–700.

Kemp, K., Savitz, B., Thompson, W., & Zanis, D. A. (2004). Developing employment services for criminal justice clients enrolled in drug user treatment programs. *Substance Use & Misuse, 39*(13/14), 2491–2511.

Kessler, R. C., Berglund, P., Delmer, O., Jin, R., Merikangas, K. R., & Walters, E. E. (2005). Lifetime prevalence and age-of-onset distributions of *DSM-IV* disorders in the National Comorbidity Survey replication. *Archives of General Psychiatry, 63,* 593–602.

Kienhuis, M., Rogers, S., Giallo, R., Matthews, J., & Treyvaud, K. (2010). A proposed model for the impact of parental fatigue on parenting adaptability and child development. *Journal of Reproductive and Infant Psychology, 28*(4), 392–402.

Klein, S. M., Giovino, G. A., Barker, D. C., Tworek, C., Cummings, K. M., & O'Connnor, R. J. (2008). Use of flavored cigarettes among older adolescents and adult smokers: United States, 2004-2005. *Nicotine Tobacco Research, 10*(7), 1209–1214.

Klonsky, E. D., & May, A. (2010). Rethinking impulsivity in suicide. *Suicide and Life-Threatening Behavior, 40*(6), 612–619.

Kuehn, B. M. (2010). Military probes epidemic of suicide. *Journal of the American Medical Association, 304,* 1427–1430.

Lamb, H. R., & Weinberger, L. E. (1998). Persons with severe mental illness in jails and prisons: A review. *Psychiatric Services, 49,* 483–492.

Latimer, W., & Zur, J. (2010). Epidemiologic trends of adolescent use of alcohol, tobacco, and other drugs. *Child and Adolescent Psychiatric Clinics of North America, 19,* 451–464.

Leddy, M., Haaga, D., Gray, J., & Schulkin, J. (2011). Postpartum mental health screening and diagnosis by obstetrician-gynecologists. *Journal of Psychosomatic Obstetrics & Gynecology, 32*(1), 27–34.

Lejano, R. P. (2006). *Frameworks for policy analysis: Merging text and context.* New York, NY: Routledge.

Lewin, T. (2010, January 26). After long decline, teenage pregnancy rate rises. *The New York Times,* p. A14.

Maier, S. E., Chen, W., & West, J. R. (1996). The effects of timing and duration of alcohol exposure on development of the fetal brain. In E. L. Abel (Ed.), *Fetal alcohol syndrome: From mechanism to prevention* (pp. 27–50). Boca Raton, FL: CRC Press.

Mann, J. J., Apter, A., Bertolote, J., Beautrais, A., Currier, D., Haas, A., . . . Hendin, H. (2005). Suicide prevention strategies: A systematic review. *Journal of American Medical Association, 294*(16), 2064–2074.

McNeal, R. B., & Hanson, W. B. (1995). An examination of strategies for gaining convergent validity in natural experiments: D.A.R.E. as an illustrative case study. *Evaluation Review, 19,* 141–158.

Mental Health America website. (2011). Retrieved from http://www.nmha.org

Miller, D. (2001, October 19). Dare reinvents itself with help from its social-scientist critics. *Chronicle of Higher Education.* Washington DC: Chronicle of Higher Education.

Miller, M., Azrael, D., & Hemenway, D. (2006). Belief in the inevitability of suicide: Results from a national survey. *Suicide and Life Threatening Behavior, 36,* 1–11.

Montoya, I. D., Carlson, J. W., & Richard, A. J. (1999). An analysis of drug abuse policies in teaching hospitals. *Journal of Behavioral Health Services & Research, 26*(1), 28–38.

Morrissey, J. P., Fagan, J. A., & Cocozza, J. J. (2009). New models of collaboration between criminal justice and mental health systems. *American Journal of Psychiatry, 166,* 1211–1214.

Mortensen, P. B., Pedersen, M. G., & Pedersen, C. B. (2010). Psychiatric family history and schizophrenia risk in Denmark: Which mental disorders are relevant? *Psychological Medicine: A Journal of Research in Psychiatry and the Allied Sciences, 40*(2), 201–210.

Mothers Against Drunk Driving. (2005). *Secrets to success.* Retrieved from http://www.madd.org/about-us/history/how-madd-has-been-successful.pdf

Mowery, W. L. (1997). Stepping up the war on drugs: Prosecution and enhanced sentences for conspiracies to possess or distribute drugs under state and federal schoolyard statutes. *Dickinson Law Review, 101*(4), 703–728.

National Association of Public Hospitals and Health Systems. (2011). Retrieved from http://www.naph.org

National Institute of Alcohol Abuse and Alcoholism. (2010). *Alcohol policy information system.* Retrieved from http://www.alcoholpolicy.niaaa.nih.gov/Home.html

National Institute of Mental Health. (2011). Retrieved from http://www.nimh.nih.gov/about/index.shtml

National Prevention, Health Promotion and Public Health Council. (2011). *National prevention strategy.* Washington, DC: Government Printing Office.

Nyre, G. F. (1985). *Final evaluation report, 1984-1985.* Los Angeles, CA: Evaluation and Training Institute.

Office of the National Drug Control Policy. (2010). *Prevention.* Retrieved from http://www.whitehouse.gov/ondcp/prevention-intro

Office of the Surgeon General. (2006). *Surgeon General's call to action to prevent and reduce underage drinking.* Retrieved from http://www.surgeongeneral.gov/topics/underagedrinking/programs.html

Palmer, K. S. (1999, Spring). A brief history: Universal health care efforts in the US. *Transcript from the Physicians for a National Health Program Spring 1999 meeting.* Retrieved from http://www.pnhp.org/facts/a_brief_history_universal_health_care_efforts_in_the_us.php?page=all

Primack, B. A., Sidani, J., Agarwal, A. A., Shadel, W. G., Donny, E. C., & Eissenberg, T. E. (2008). Prevalence and associations with waterpipe tobacco smoking among U.S. university students. *Annals of Behavioral Medicine, 36*(1), 81–86.

Research and Development Corporation. (2010). *The war within: Preventing suicide in the US military.* Arlington, VA: Author.

Richardson, A. K., Green, M., Xiao, H., Sokol, K., & Vallone, N. (2010). Evidence for truth®: The young adult response to youth-focused anti-smoking media campaign. *American Journal of Preventative Medicine, 39*(6), 500–506.

Ringwalt, C., Ennett, S. T., & Holt, K. D. (1990). *An outcome evaluation of D.A.R.E. (Drug Abuse Resistance Education).* Raleigh, NC: Research Triangle Institute.

Ringwalt, C., Hanley, S., Vincus, A. A., Ennett, S. T., Rohrbach, L. A., & Bowling, J. M. (2008). The prevalence of effective substance abuse prevention curricula in the nation's high schools. *Journal of Primary Prevention, 29,* 479–488.

Ringwalt, C. L., Clark, H. K., Hanley, S., Shamblen, S. R., & Flewelling, R. L. (2010). The effects of project ALERT one year past curriculum completion. *Prevention Science, 11*(2), 172–184.

Robertson, E., Celasun, N., & Stewart, D. E. (2003). Risk factors for postpartum depression. In D. E. Stewart, E. Robertson, C. L. Dennis, S. L. Grace, & T. Wallington (Eds.), *Postpartum depression: Literature review of risk factors and interventions.* Toronto, Ontario, Canada: University Health Network Women's Health Program for Toronto Public Health.

Robertson, E., Grace, S., Wallington, T., & Stewart, D. E., (2004). Antenatal risk factors for postpartum depression: A synthesis of recent literature. *General Hospital Psychiatry: Psychiatry medicine and Primary Care, 26*(4), 289–295.

Robinson, W. M., & Unrah, B. T. (2008). The hepatitis experiments at the Willowbrook School. In E. J. Emanuel, C. Grady, R. A. Crouch, R. K. Liw, F. G. Miller, &

D. Wendler (Eds.), *The Oxford textbook of clinical research ethics* (pp. 80–85). Oxford, England: Oxford University Press.

Rohde, P., Lewinsohn, P. M., Kahler, C. W., Seeley, J. R., & Brown, R. A. (2001). Natural course of alcohol use disorders from adolescence to young adulthood. *Journal of the American Academy of Child & Adolescent Psychiatry, 40,* 83–90.

Rosenbaum, D. P., & Hanson, G. S. (1998). Assessing the effects of school-based drug education: A six-year multi-level analysis of Project D.A.R.E. *Journal of Research in Crime and Delinquency, 35,* 381–412.

Ross, J. S. (2002). The committee on the cost of medical care and the history of health insurance in the United States. *Einstein Quarterly Journal of Biology and Medicine, 19,* 129–134.

Sawdi, H. (1999). Individual risk factors for adolescent substance use. *Drug and Alcohol Dependence, 55*(3), 209–224.

Schmidt, J. D., & Sherman, L. W. (1993). Does arrest deter domestic violence? *American Behavioral Scientist, 36,* 601–609.

Seiden, R. (1978). Where are they now? A follow-up study of suicide attempters from the Golden Gate Bridge. *Suicide and Life Threatening Behavior, 8,* 203–216.

Senate Report 105-48, 105th Congress, 1st Session, 154 (1997).

Shain, B. N., & the Committee on Adolescence. (2007). Suicide and suicide attempts in adolescents. *Pediatrics, 120*(3), 669–676.

Sherman, L. W., & Berk, R. A. (1984). The specific deterrent effects of arrest for domestic assault. *American Sociological Review, 49,* 261–272.

Shuster, E. (1997). Fifty years later: The significance of the Nuremberg Code. *New England Journal of Medicine, 336,* 1436–1440.

Silagy, C., Lancaster, T., Stead, L., Mant, D., & Fowler, G. (2004). *Nicotine replacement therapy for smoking cessation (Review).* Hoboken, NJ: Wiley.

Silvia, E. S., Thorne, J., & Tashjian, C. (1997). *School-based drug prevention programs: A longitudinal study in selected school districts.* Research Triangle Park, NC: Research Triangle Institute.

Simmons, P. L. (1999). Solving the nation's drug problem: Drug courts signal a move towards therapeutic jurisprudence. *Gonzaga Law Review, 35*(2), 237–264.

Slater, M. D., Kelley, K. J., Lawrence, F. R., Stanley, L. R., & Comello, M. L. G. (2011). Assessing media campaigns linking marijuana non-use with autonomy and aspirations: "Be Under Your Own Influence" and ONDCP's "Above the Influence." *Prevention Science, 12*(1), 12–22.

Sloboda, Z., Stephens, R. C., Stephens, P. C., Grey, S. F., Teasdale, B., Hawthorne, R. D., . . . Marquette, J. F. (2009). The adolescent substance abuse prevention study: A randomized field trial of a universal substance abuse prevention program. *Drug and Alcohol Dependence, 102,* 1–10.

State of Washington Department of Social and Health Services. (2006). *Process evaluation of Bright Start Demonstration Program's implementation.* Portland, OR: ECONorthwest. Retrieved from http://www.econw.com/reports/welfare 6960.pdf

Stenbacka, M. (2003). Problematic alcohol and cannabis use in adolescence— Risk of serious adult substance abuse? *Drug and Alcohol Review, 22*(3), 277–286.

Stevens, R. A., Rosenberg, C. E., & Burns, L. R. (2006). *Putting the past back in: History and health policy in the United States.* New Brunswick, NJ: Rutgers University Press.

Stokey, E., & Zeckhauser, R. (1978). *A primer for policy analysis.* New York, NY: W. W. Norton.

Strickland, C. J., Walsh, E., & Cooper, M. (2006). Healing fractured families: Parents' and elders' perspectives on the impact of colonization and youth suicide prevention in a Pacific Northwest American Indian tribe. *Journal of Transcultural Nursing, 17*(1), 5–12.

Substance Abuse Mental Health Services Administration. (2010). Health reform: Overview of the Affordable Care Act. *SAMHSA News, 18,* 1–20.

Suvisaari, J. (2010). Risk factors of schizophrenia. *Duodecim, 126*(3), 869–876.

Thombs, D. L. (2006). *Introduction to addictive behaviors* (3rd ed.). New York, NY: Guilford Press.

Trenholm, C., Devaney, B., Fortson, K., Clark, M., Quay, L., & Wheeler, J. (2008). Impacts of abstinence education on teen sexual activity, risk of pregnancy, and risk of sexually transmitted diseases. *Journal of Policy Analysis and Management, 27, 255–276.*

Universal Pictures. (2007). Policy regarding tobacco depiction in films. Retrieved from http://www.universalpictures.com/legal/tobacco/index.html

U.S. Department of Agriculture. (2011). *Food and nutrition assistance.* Retrieved from http://www.ers.usda.gov/Browse/view.aspx?subject=FoodNutrition Assistance

U.S. Department of Education, NY State Archives. (2011). *Federal education policy and the states, 1945-2009: The Ford years: Legislative history—P.L. 94-142.* Albany, NY: Author. Retrieved from http://www.sifepp.nysed.gov/edpolicy/research/res_essay_ford_pl94_142_doubts.shtml

U.S. Department of Health and Human Services. (2010). *Grounds for involuntary termination of parental rights.* Retrieved from http://www.childwelfare.gov/systemwide/laws_policies/statutes/groundtermin.cfm

U.S. Department of Health and Human Services. (2011). *Advancing the health, safety and well-being of our people: FY 2011 President's Budget for HHS.* Washington, DC: Author. Retrieved from http://www.hhs.gov/asfr/ob/docbudget/2011budgetinbrief.pdf

U.S. Department of Health and Human Services, Centers for Medicare and Medicaid Services. (2011). *Your guide to Medicare's prevention services.* Washington, DC: Government Printing Office.

U.S. Department of Health and Human Services, Office of Child Support Enforcement. (2010). *Child support enforcement FY 2008 annual report to Congress.* Washington, DC: Author. Retrieved from http://www.acf.hhs.gov/programs/cse/pubs/2011/reports/fy2008_annual_report

U.S. Department of Health and Human Services, Office of the Surgeon General. (2000). *The surgeon general's call to action to reduce tobacco use.* Retrieved from http://web.archive.org/web/20070427164350/http://www.cdc.gov/tobacco/data_statistics/sgr/sgr_2000/highlights/highlight_advertising.htm

U.S. Department of Health and Human Services, Office of the Surgeon General. (2005). *Advisory on alcohol use in pregnancy.* Retrieved from http://www.surgeongeneral.gov/pressreleases/sg02222005.html

U.S. Department of Health and Human Services, Office of the Surgeon General. (2007). *The Surgeon General's call to action to prevent and reduce underage drinking.* Retrieved from http://www.surgeongeneral.gov/topics/underage drinking/goals.html

U.S. Government Accountability Office. (1997). *Drug control: Observations on elements of the Federal Drug Control Strategy* (GAO/GGD-97-42). Washington, DC: Government Printing Office.

U.S. Government Accountability Office. (2003). *Youth illicit drug use prevention: DARE long-term evaluations and federal efforts to identify effective programs* (GAO-03-172R). Washington, DC: Government Printing Office.

U.S. Public Health Services. (1999). *Suicide prevention scientific information: Risk and protective factors.* Retrieved from http://www.cdc.gov/ncipc/dvp/suicide/Suicide-risk-p-factors.htm

W., B. (1996). *The A.A. service manual.* New York, NY: Alcoholics Anonymous World Services.

Wagenaar, A. C., Salois, M. J., & Komoro, K. A. (2009). Effects of beverage alcohol price and tax levels on drinking: A meta-analysis of 1003 estimates from 112 studies. *Addiction, 104* (2), 179–190.

Weimer, D. L., & Vining, A. R. (2011). *Policy analysis.* New York, NY: Longman.

Weiss, C., Murphy-Graham, E., Petrosino, A., & Gandhi, A. G. (2008). The fairy godmother-and her wants: Making the dream of evidence-based policy come true. *American Journal of Evaluation, 29,* 29–47.

West, S. L., & O'Neal, K. K. (2004). Project D.A.R.E. outcome effectiveness revisited. *American Journal of Public Health, 94,* 1027–1029.

World Federation for Mental Health. (2011). Retrieved from http://www.wfmh.org

World Health Organization. (2011). Retrieved from http://www.who.int

Zernike, K. (2001, February 1). Antidrug program says it will adopt a new strategy. *The New York Times,* pp. 1.

Index_____

About the Authors _____

Maureen A. Pirog taught in the Finance Department of the Wharton Business School at the University of Pennsylvania before joining the faculty in the School of Public and Environment Affairs at IU in 1983, where she is the Rudy Professor of Policy Analysis. She is the founder and director of the IU Institute for Family and Social Responsibility, a multidisciplinary, multicampus institute that provides research expertise and technical assistance to state and national social service organizations. Dr. Pirog also has an affiliated appointment as a Professor at the Daniel J. Evans School of Public Affairs at the University of Washington. She is the editor in chief of the *Journal of Policy Analysis and Management*, the top ranked journal in the field of public administration. Professor Pirog is an expert in the methodology of policy analysis and her research focuses on a broad range of social policy issues. She received a BA and an MA in economics from Boston College in 1975 and a PhD in public policy analysis from the University of Pennsylvania in 1981.

Emily M. Good is a practicing therapist in Bloomington, Indiana, working with children, adolescents, and families. She received a BA in psychology from Indiana University (IU) in 2008 and an MS in counseling psychology from IU in 2012.

⑤SAGE research**methods**

The essential online tool for researchers from the world's leading methods publisher

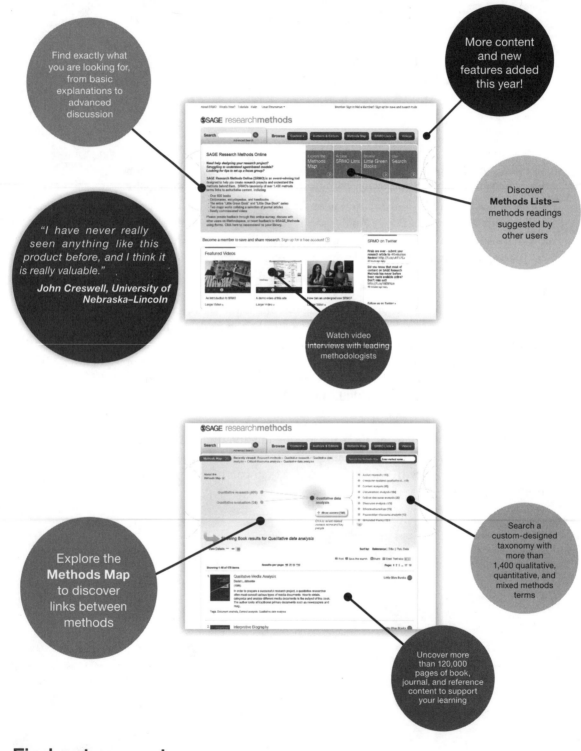

Find exactly what you are looking for, from basic explanations to advanced discussion

More content and new features added this year!

"*I have never really seen anything like this product before, and I think it is really valuable.*"

John Creswell, University of Nebraska–Lincoln

Discover **Methods Lists**— methods readings suggested by other users

Watch video interviews with leading methodologists

Explore the **Methods Map** to discover links between methods

Search a custom-designed taxonomy with more than 1,400 qualitative, quantitative, and mixed methods terms

Uncover more than 120,000 pages of book, journal, and reference content to support your learning

Find out more at
www.sageresearchmethods.com